BEATING OBAMACARE

BEATING OBAMACARE

Your Handbook for Surviving the New Health Care Law

BETSY McCAUGHEY, Ph.D.

Cataloging-in-Publication data on file with the Library of Congress
ISBN 978-1-62157-079-0

Published in the United States by
Regnery Publishing, Inc.
One Massachusetts Avenue NW
Washington, DC 20001
www.Regnery.com

Some material in this book appeared previously in electronic form in the ebook *Decoding the Obama Health Law: What You Need to Know* published in 2012 by Paperless Publishing LLC, 609 Greenwich Street, New York, NY 10014.

This is the first Regnery edition, published in 2013

Manufactured in the United States of America
20 19 18 17 16 15 14

Books are available in quantity for promotional or premium use. Write to Director of Special Sales, Regnery Publishing, Inc., One Massachusetts Avenue NW, Washington, DC 20001, for information on discounts and terms, or call (202) 216-0600.

Distributed to the trade by
Perseus Distribution
250 West 57th Street
New York, NY 10107

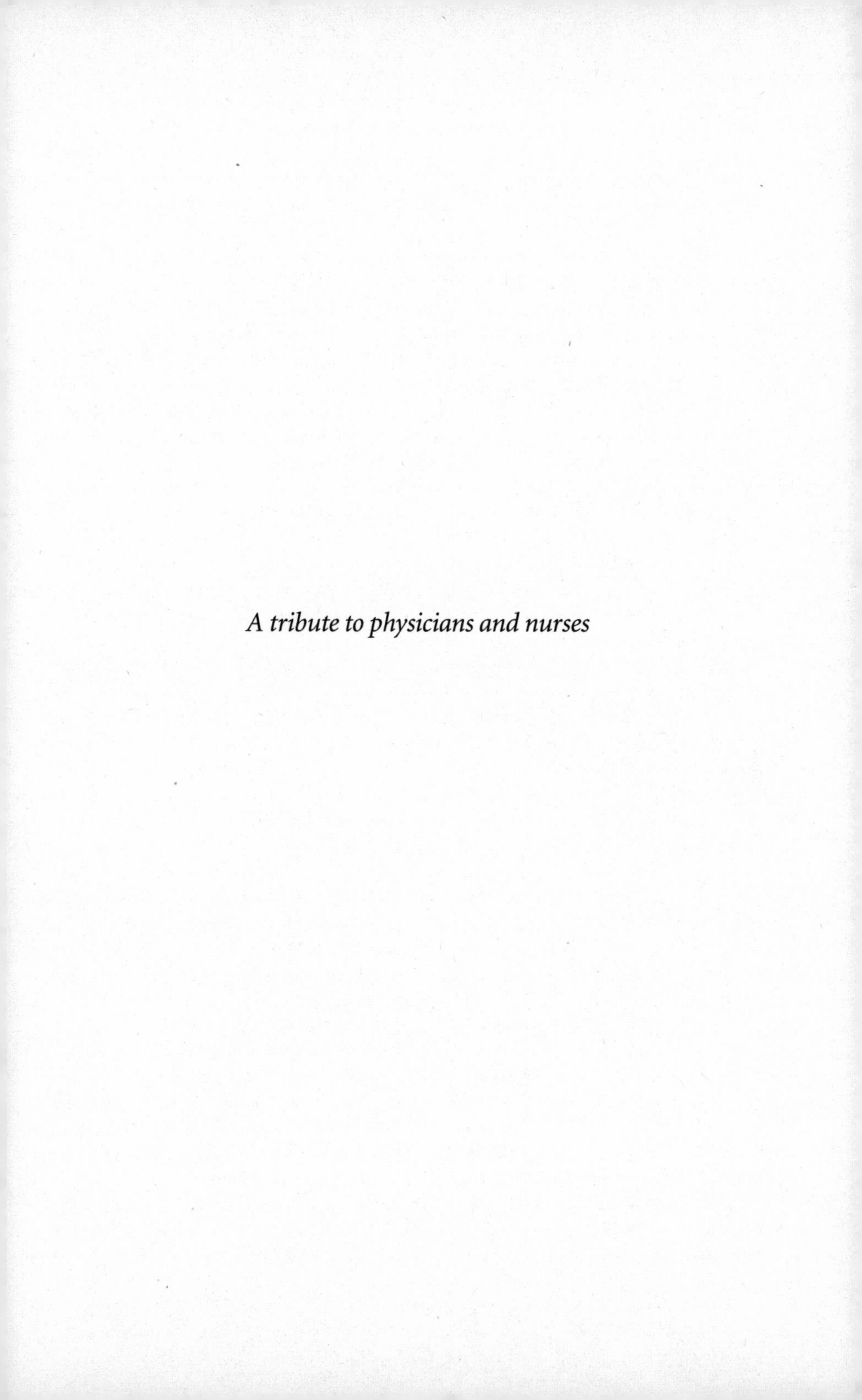

A tribute to physicians and nurses

CONTENTS

CHAPTER ONE

OBAMACARE IS HERE TO STAY

Did you know?

- Many Americans who now get health insurance through their job could lose their coverage in 2014
- The employer mandate adds $1.79 per hour to the cost of hiring a full-time worker
- As of 2014, you'll have to show the IRS proof of insurance when you file your taxes
- Under Obamacare, for the first time in history, the federal government will dictate how doctors treat privately insured patients

Barack Obama's re-election and Democratic gains in the U.S. Senate end any possibility of repealing the Obama health law in the near future. The health care law will roll out as written, imposing major changes on you, your family, and your job. If you are currently uninsured because you can't afford it, help may be on the way. But if you are one of the 250 million Americans who are already covered, you may be losing that coverage soon.

The Thursday before the election, registered nurses at the Alta Bates Summit Medical Center in Oakland, California, struck to protest bigger workloads and lower benefits. A hospital spokesperson explained that the Obama health law makes the nursing cuts necessary. "Medicare is reducing reimbursement. We have to change the way we operate."[1] Meanwhile, in Florida, Darden Restaurants, owners of Olive Garden, Red Lobster, and other chains, says it will shift full-time workers to part-time status to evade the Obamacare requirement that employers cover full-time workers with a costly health insurance plan. All across the country doctors, hospitals, and businesses are acting quickly to soften the impact of the Obama health law. You need to know what is ahead and what you can do to protect yourself, your family, and your job.

If you currently get your health insurance through a job, you may lose it as of January 1, 2014. That is when the new "employer mandate" goes into effect, requiring employers with fifty or more full-time workers to provide the government-designed health plan or pay a fine. The government plan is so expensive, it adds $1.79 per hour to the cost of a full-time employee.[2] That's incidental if you're hiring neurosurgeons, but a hefty increase in the cost of hiring busboys and sales clerks. Currently employers in retail and fast food industries pay less than half that to cover their workers. To avoid the costly mandate, some employers will opt for the fine, while others will push workers into part-time status. Either way, workers lose their on-the-job coverage.

Worse, they risk losing their full-time jobs. Even the fine adds 98 cents an hour to the cost of labor, enough to make some employers cut back on hours or lay off employees.

Only in Washington, D.C., could an employer mandate result in workers losing coverage and maybe their jobs. One third of employers are considering canceling coverage, according to McKinsey & Company management consultants.[3] But that doesn't mean you'll be uninsured. You won't have that choice.

When you file your taxes, you will have to show proof that you are enrolled in the one-size-fits-all plan approved by the federal government. It's mandatory, starting January 1, 2014—or the IRS will withhold your refund. If you've been going without insurance, or your employer drops coverage, your options will be enrolling in Medicaid (if you're eligible) or buying a government-approved health plan on your state health exchange.

What is an insurance exchange? It's like a supermarket that sells only cereal. The exchanges will sell only the government-designed plan. In most states, exchanges will have an 800 number, a website, and a government office like the DMV. People with household incomes up to $92,200 will be eligible for a subsidy.

If you're a senior or a baby boomer, expect less care than in the past. Cuts to future Medicare funding will pay for more than half the Obama health law. Hospitals, for example, will have $247 billion less to care for the same number of seniors than if the law had not passed. So hospitals will spread nurses thinner. California nurses already are striking over the increased workloads. When Medicare cuts caused hospitals to reduce nursing care in the past, elderly patients had a lower chance of surviving their stay, and death rates from heart attacks rose.[4]

For the first time in history, the federal government will control how doctors treat privately insured patients. Section 1311 of the law empowers the Secretary of Health and Human Services to standardize what doctors do. Even if you have a private plan from Cigna or Aetna and you paid for it yourself, the federal government will have some say over your doctors' decisions—with an eye to reducing health care consumption.

If you sell your house and make a profit, you could be paying a new 3.8 percent tax on the gain. Obamacare includes about half a trillion dollars in tax hikes. One that many people still don't know about is the 3.8 percent additional tax on gains from selling any asset, including your home, small business, stocks, or bonds, effective January 1, 2013. The new tax is on top of capital gains taxes, and it applies to any gain that pushes your income over $200,000. (Homeowners selling a primary residence may be excluded under some circumstances.)

These are just a few of the hundreds of changes that will affect you, your family, and your job. You could wade through the 2,572-page Obama health law yourself. But if you have a better way to spend the next three months of your life, you can rely on this guide instead. It will help you understand what the law says—and the thousands of additional regulations being written right now.

The Obama administration is adding federal workers at a rapid pace to churn out these additional regulations and enforce them. The government's own projections say health care administration—paying bureaucrats to tell doctors and patients what to do—will soar from the $29 billion it cost when President Obama was first elected to $71 billion by 2020. Forty billion dollars a year more in bureaucracy. What a shame. And what an irony. That's enough money to buy private health plans for fully half of all Americans who are currently uninsured because they can't afford it.

Thousands of new regulations have already been written to control what you, your doctor, and your employer can do. To help you survive this avalanche of new rules, I've prepared this simple guide.

CHAPTER TWO

DECODING THE OBAMA HEALTH LAW

Did you know?

- The Obama health law is 2,572 pages. Most members of Congress didn't read it before voting on it
- The law is stuffed with hard-to-follow references to dozens of other pieces of legislation
- Obamacare changes the way everyone in America gets health care

If you're clueless about the Obama health law, you're not alone. Most people have heard the political bickering and supercharged rhetoric, but they don't know what the law actually says.

But you'll need to know soon, because this law will affect you and your entire family. The new health law is not just about helping the uninsured (a worthy goal). Obamacare will change how everyone in America gets medical care. It will even regulate the decisions your doctor can make. You haven't felt the effects yet, but you will.

One reason for the political rancor over this new law is that so few people—including even members of Congress—have read it. The law is a nearly unreadable 2,572 pages. Why so long? The framers of the U.S. Constitution created the entire federal government in just eighteen pages. If only the Washington bigwigs of today showed the same restraint.

In addition to the law's length, its obfuscating language gives readers the runaround. Who could understand this gobbledygook?

Here's a typical passage from the Obama health law:

> 1) Subparagraph (B) of section 6724(d)(1) of the Internal Revenue Code of 1986 (relating to definitions), as amended by Section 1502, is amended by striking "or" at the end of clause (xxiii), by striking "and" at the end of clause (xxiv) and inserting "or" and by inserting after clause (xxiv) the following new clause:

"(xxv) section 6056 (relating to returns relating to large employers required to report on health coverage), and".

2) Paragraph (2) of section 6724(d) of such Code, as so amended, is amended by striking "or" at the end of subparagraph (FF), by striking the period at the end of subparagraph (GG) and inserting " or" and by inserting after subparagraph (GG) the following new subparagraph:

(HH) section 6056 c (relating to statements relating to large employers required to report on health insurance coverage).

The legalese you just read is from Section 6056 of the act, requiring large employers to report the insurance coverage they provide for each employee.

To even begin to comprehend this one section of the law, you'd have to consult dozens of other pieces of legislation to cobble the meaning together. Yet employers who fail to follow the provisions could face thousands of dollars of fines.

This guide decodes what the Obama health law says, and tells you, based on the Obama administration's own financial projections, how it will probably affect you. No spin, no partisanship, just a translation into plain honest English. I've read the whole unwieldy and misleading law and summarized it for you here.

This guide tells you what you will have to do to comply. So let's get started. If you come across an unfamiliar word or phrase, be sure to consult the Obamacare Glossary at the end of the guide.

CHAPTER THREE

THE OBAMACARE TIMELINE

Did you know?

- Obamacare contains twenty new taxes or tax hikes, the first of which went into effect in 2010
- In January 2014, all Americans are required to have health insurance or pay a penalty
- In 2018, the Independent Payment Advisory Board has the power to further cut what Medicare will spend on seniors

March 2010

President Obama signs the Patient Protection and Affordable Care Act into law.

States file lawsuits challenging the constitutionality of the law.

July 2010

The first of twenty new taxes and tax hikes goes into effect—a tax on tanning salons.

September 2010

Early provisions require insurers to

- eliminate co-pays for preventive care (the cost is included in your premium instead),
- cover young adults on their parent's plan, and
- stop selling mini-med plans that cap the dollar amounts paid for care.

January 2011

"Donut Hole" begins to close for Medicare Part D.
New penalties for HSA disbursements kick in.
New fees on pharmaceutical companies start.
New taxes on medical devices begin.

June 2012

The United States Supreme Court rules most of the Obama health law constitutional, but says each state can decide whether or not to expand Medicaid.

January 2013

Medicare Part A payroll tax hike and new 3.8 percent unearned income tax go into effect.

January 2014

All Americans are required to have insurance or pay a penalty.

Employers with fifty or more workers are required to provide insurance or pay a penalty.

January 2018

Independent Payment Advisory Board (IPAB) reduces spending on seniors.

"Cadillac tax" penalizes generous health plans.

CHAPTER FOUR

WINNERS AND LOSERS

Did you know?

- Nurses face layoffs, and nursing care will be spread thinner when the Obama health law cuts what hospitals are paid to care for seniors
- Union members and other people with generous health plans risk losing them in 2018
- Government spending on health care administration—telling doctors and patients what to do—will more than double in the next decade

Winners

Low-income childless adults who were not eligible for Medicaid under the old rules may be eligible in 2014 in states that choose to expand Medicaid eligibility.

Households earning up to $92,200 for a family of four who pay for their own insurance. As of 2014, they will get a subsidy funded by taxpayers.

Young adults, who are now eligible to stay on their parent's health plan until age twenty-six.

Newcomers to the U.S. The law expands programs to serve people of diverse languages and cultures, regardless of immigration status.

Racial and ethnic minorities will benefit from federally funded programs to train a diverse health care workforce and from numerous "community transformation grants" targeted explicitly at minority organizations.

Government employees are winners. Obamacare is causing the federal government to add workers at a rapid pace. Federal actuaries predict that government spending on health care administration—bureaucrats telling patients and doctors what to do—will soar from $29 billion in 2008 to more than $71 billion in 2020.

Insurance companies are both winners and losers. They are guaranteed customers. The law forces you to buy their product. But on February 29, 2012, Secretary of Health and Human Services Kathleen Sebelius told Congress the private insurance market is in a "death spiral."[1] Blame Obamacare's costly regulations.

Chronically ill patients are winners and losers. They will benefit from rules barring insurers from putting lifetime caps on their care. But they will be vulnerable to the impact of funding cuts to hospitals and dialysis centers.

Losers

Nurses and other hospital employees will lose out. Hospitals will face severe budgetary pressures, warns Chief Actuary Richard Foster, because of cuts in Medicare reimbursement. In the past, when Medicare cut payments to hospitals, nursing care was spread thinner, and nursing workloads increased.

Hospital patients will wait longer when cutbacks reduce the supply of diagnostic equipment and fewer nurses are on the floor.

Taxpayers who earn more than $200,000, or $250,000 per couple are hit with higher Medicare Part A payroll taxes and a new 3.8 percent tax on unearned income in addition to the capital gains tax.

Union members and other people with generous health plans will risk losing them in 2018, when a 40 percent "Cadillac tax" on insurers offering these plans begins.

Doctors can expect lower pay, more paperwork, and more government interference in how they treat their patients.

Seniors pay for more than half the Obama health law through cuts in Medicare and Medicare Advantage programs. They will get less care than if the law hadn't passed. Baby boomers will enter Medicare in record numbers over the next decade. They will also get less care than if the law had not passed.

Women (and men) who want to keep their medical records private will find it hard to do so. Privacy advocates claim the law will compel Americans to share "with millions of strangers who are not physicians confidential private and personal medical history information they do not wish to share."[2] Women make the health decisions in most families. But the law gives the Secretary of Health and Human Services the power to decide what your health plan covers, how much it can cost, and even what your doctor can do.

CHAPTER FIVE

THE INDIVIDUAL MANDATE

Did you know?

- Your current health insurance may not meet the Obamacare requirements
- If you aren't enrolled in a "qualified plan," the IRS can withhold your tax refund
- Your doctor's decisions will be monitored for compliance with federal guidelines

No part of Obamacare is more controversial than the "individual mandate." For the first time in history, the federal government is requiring most Americans to buy a product—in this case, health insurance.

Section 1501 of the Obama health law requires nearly everyone to enroll in a one-size-fits-all, government-designed health insurance plan. It's called a "qualified plan." It can be sold by a private insurance company such as Aetna or Cigna, a regional insurer in your part of the country, or a not-for-profit. Or it can be coverage provided by a big employer that self-insures. But to be "qualified," the plan has to include what the federal government deems "essential benefits." The power to decide those benefits is in the hands of a presidential appointee, the Secretary of Health and Human Services.

For example, nothing in the actual Obamacare law guarantees that health plans must pay for contraception, a recent hot-button issue. But President Barack Obama and his HHS Secretary have decreed that all health plans must cover it. And a future occupant of the White House could decree just the opposite.

The individual mandate goes into effect in 2014. To avoid paying a penalty, you must be enrolled in a qualified plan that year. Where will you find a "qualified plan"? Most Americans currently get their insurance through a job—their own job, or a spouse's or a parent's. If you get your insurance that way, the employer will be making a crucial decision sometime in 2013 on whether to adjust your insurance plan to meet the new federal standards or to stop offering insurance altogether. Estimates on how many employers will stop offering coverage vary from 8 to 33 percent.

If you don't get your insurance through a job, or if you do, but your employer discontinues it in 2014, you'll be enrolling in Medicaid or buying a "qualified plan" on a state insurance exchange. These brand-new exchanges will generally have government-run websites, toll free numbers, and DMV-like offices. You may also try going to an insurance broker—though brokers may become scarce. This guide will walk you through all these options.

On the state insurance exchange, you'll be enrolling in a Bronze, Silver, Gold, or Platinum plan. Don't be fooled by the names. This isn't like going to Tiffany's. All these glittery sounding plans offer the same "essential benefits." Only the co-pays and deductibles differ. Gold and Platinum plans make you pay more up front in your premium but allow lower co-pays and deductibles.

Keep in mind that if you currently buy your own insurance, your plan may not meet the standard of a "qualified plan." High-deductible plans certainly won't. Private insurance companies are busy revamping their plans to conform to the government blueprint.

Penalties

When you file your taxes, you will have to attach proof that you are enrolled in a "qualified plan." Employers who cover their workers and families will send this proof along with the W-2. State exchanges and insurance brokers can also give you a receipt to prove that you are in the required plan. If you don't provide proof, the law gives the IRS new powers to penalize you.

The penalties take effect in 2014. If you don't enroll in a "qualified plan" and prove that you were in it for at least ten months of that year (being uninsured for less than three months isn't punishable) you will have to pay either a flat fee of $95 or one percent of your gross income (up to $285), whichever is higher.

After 2014, the penalty gets steeper until it reaches a flat fee of $695 for an individual (three times that for a family) or 2.5 percent of your gross income (to a maximum of $2085), whichever is higher, in 2016. The law empowers the IRS to seize tax refunds as payment toward an unpaid penalty. Section 5000A of the Internal Revenue Code expressly states that you cannot be criminally prosecuted for failing to pay the penalty.

Some groups are exempt from the mandate:

- If you are already enrolled in government programs such as Medicare, you are considered covered
- American Indians receive health insurance in a separate program and are considered covered
- Prisoners
- Members of the armed services and their families

- Certain religious groups
- If you don't qualify for Medicaid and can prove financial hardship
- Illegal immigrants
- Young adults (under thirty) are not exempt but can meet the requirement for a "qualified plan" by enrolling in a catastrophic insurance plan that is not available to adults thirty and over

Government Controls on Your Care

The individual mandate is just what the word "mandate" means. It's compulsory. Enrolling in a "qualified plan" will shield you from the IRS penalty but it will also mean the federal government has new control over your medical care and the decisions your doctor makes. For the first time in history, this law empowers the federal government to control how doctors treat privately insured patients. So even if you have your own private health plan that you paid for yourself, the federal government will have some say over your care.

Section 1311 (h)(1) of the law says that you have to be in a "qualified plan," and "qualified plans" can pay only doctors and hospitals that follow the dictates of the federal government. The new law says that the Secretary of Health and Human Services, appointed by the president, can impose any regulation to improve health care "quality." That could be everything in medicine—whether your cardiologist recommends a stent versus a bypass, or when your obstetrician performs a Caesarean.

Your doctor will have to enter your treatments into an electronic database, your doctor's decisions will be monitored for compliance with federal guidelines, and ultimately your doctor may have to choose between doing what's right for you and avoiding a government penalty. The new federal oversight will standardize medical practice with an eye to reducing consumption of medical care.

Privacy

There is cause for great concern on the issue of who will see your medical records. Mark Rothstein, a University of Louisville School of Medicine bioethicist, worries that the new federal system will disclose too much. Rothstein warns that every doctor you see will have access to all your medical records. Your oral surgeon doesn't need to know about your bout with depression or your erectile dysfunction, but will see it.[1] On May 31, 2011, the Health and Human Services Department proposed allowing patients to request a report on who has electronically viewed their information. Unfortunately, that would be after the fact.

Paying for Your Mandatory Insurance

Obamacare creates two new entitlements to make the mandatory purchase of insurance less onerous.

New Entitlements under Obamacare: $1,683 Trillion through 2020

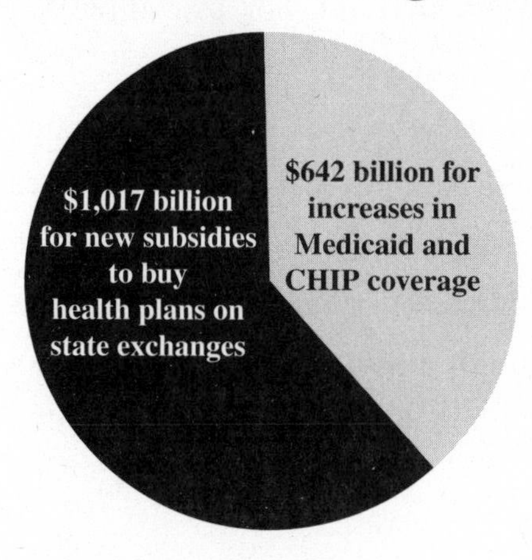

Source: Congressional Budget Office, July 2012

First, the law vastly expands who is eligible for Medicaid. The new law throws open the Medicaid doors in any state that adopts the new, looser federal rules. A family of four with a household income up to $30,657 (2012 level) will qualify for Medicaid in states that implement the expansion. Childless adults, who were ineligible for Medicaid in most states, will become eligible. The president often promised that he would solve the problem of the uninsured by making health plans more affordable. But that is not what the law does. Instead, most Americans who are currently uninsured because they can't afford it will be going onto Medicaid in 2014. Also, some low-paid workers who currently are insured through work will lose that coverage in 2014 and land on Medicaid. Estimates vary widely on how many people will be dropped in 2014 by employers who decide that providing "essential benefits" costs too much.

One caveat here: the United States Supreme Court ruled on June 28, 2012, that states do not have to go along with the Medicaid expansion. Texas and several other states have already declared that they won't expand Medicaid. So you need to keep your eyes open for local news or call local officials to find out what your state will be doing.

Subsidies on the Exchange

For more affluent households, the law creates subsidies to help pay the cost of insurance bought on a state exchange. The subsidy is paid directly to the insurer to reduce your premium. By 2019, households earning up to $100,000 will be eligible for these health care handouts paid for by taxpayers. These subsidies will be available to almost any legal resident of the U.S. You do not have to have been previously uninsured. There are no asset tests. You can own new cars, a home, even a castle, and still qualify. Newcomers to the U.S. qualify for subsidies on the exchanges, without a waiting period, as long as they enter the country legally.

By 2019, the individual mandate and the two new entitlements will transform the health care landscape. According to the government's actuaries, half of all health care spending will be paid for by government. Of course, "paid for by government" is a myth. The new entitlements are funded by raising taxes and taking funds from Medicare.

To learn more about options for complying with the individual mandate, turn to the chapters below on "Getting Your Insurance through Work," "The Health Insurance Exchange," and "Medicaid Nation."

CHAPTER SIX

GETTING YOUR INSURANCE THROUGH WORK—IT'S GOING TO GET HARDER AND HARDER

Did you know?

- One third of employers are considering dropping health insurance for employees because of Obamacare's costs
- You will have to tell your employer how much your spouse makes
- Young entry-level workers will be priced out of full-time jobs

Most Americans get their health insurance through a job—their own, their spouse's, or a parent's. Employers voluntarily offer insurance in order to attract the best workforce and do the right thing.

Health Insurance in America before Obamacare's Full Implementation (in Millions)

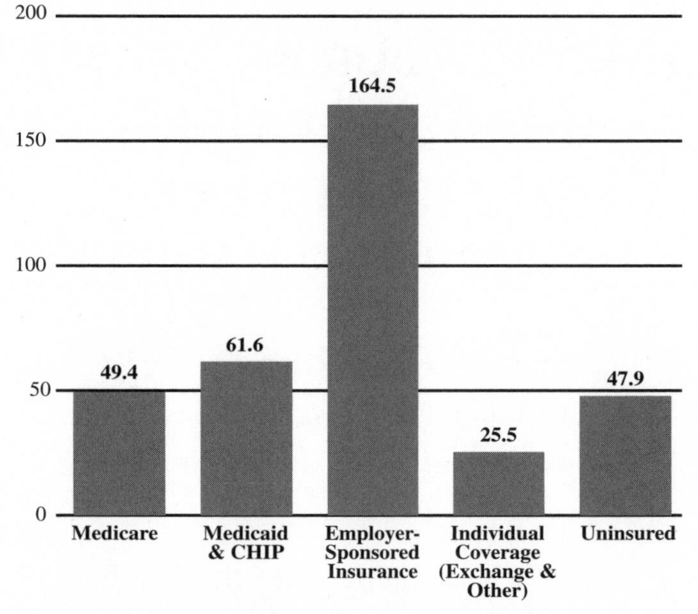

Source: Richard Foster, April 22, 2010, memorandum, "Estimated Financial Effects of 'Patient Protection and Affordable Care Act' as Amended," submitted as the basis for Foster's testimony before the House Subcommittee on Health

But if you have insurance at work, you may lose it in 2014. According to McKinsey & Company, a management consulting firm, one third of employers are already considering dropping coverage for employees and their families when the employer mandate goes into effect. McKinsey found that among employers who have actually studied the new law, the figure is even higher.[1]

That doesn't mean you will be uninsured. You won't have that choice. The IRS will require you to have insurance and attach proof of it when you file your federal income taxes. If your employer drops coverage in 2014, you will have to find an insurance broker, buy a plan on a state insurance exchange, or downgrade to Medicaid if you qualify.

Here are the facts about Section 1513 of the Obama health law—called "Employer Responsibility."

The employer mandate requires that employers with fifty or more full-time workers must provide health coverage or pay a penalty. And not just any coverage, but a package of expensive benefits that the administration deems "essential."

In most states, the mandate will add $1.79 per hour to the cost of a full-time employee,[2] and in New York and New Jersey (where health plans are more expensive), it will add a whopping $2 an hour or more, according to economist James Sherk of the Heritage Foundation.[3] This is the biggest government-imposed labor-cost hike in American history.

Even employers who currently offer coverage voluntarily will be clobbered. They lose leeway about what benefits to offer and how much to ask workers to contribute. Your employer may very well decide that paying the

$2,000 per employee annual fine is cheaper and easier than complying with the mandate.

The devil is in the details:

1. One of the earliest provisions, effective September 2010, prohibited mini-med plans. The philosophy behind these plans was that some coverage is better than no coverage. They were commonly offered by retailers, fast food companies, and other industries that employ large numbers of modestly paid workers. Mini-med plans cap what the insurer has to pay out if you get sick, with an annual cap and a lifetime cap. Obamacare seeks to eliminate these caps. Employers who offered mini-meds (or who still do, with a special waiver from the Obama administration) will be hit with much higher costs when they have to provide the mandated plan.
2. Employers can no longer reward top managers or most-valued employees with fancier health insurance. The same plan must be offered to all employees, for the sake of equality.
3. As of 2014, employers who don't provide coverage will be fined as soon as an

employee applies for Medicaid or a subsidy on the state insurance exchange. The fine will be calculated on the total number of employees minus thirty. So a business with fifty workers that doesn't provide insurance will be fined $2,000 x (50 - 30) = $40,000. If the business employs a hundred people instead of fifty, the fine will be $140,000. In calculating the fine, it doesn't matter how many employees apply for taxpayer subsidies or Medicaid. The fine is calculated on the business's *total* number of employees.

4. To provide insurance that is "affordable" according to the government's definition, employers will have to ask for a lot of personal information, including who you are living with and how much each member of your household earns. You may not want to tell your boss what your husband makes, but you will have to. The new law says employers must provide *affordable* insurance. They can ask workers to chip in, but the worker contribution cannot amount to more than 9.5 percent of *household* income. That means what you, your spouse, and anyone else in your family earn. The insurance could be affordable for you but not for the co-worker

whose spouse earns less. If the employee contribution exceeds 9.5 percent of the household income of that employee, making it unaffordable, and the employee goes to the insurance exchange for a subsidized plan instead, the employer gets fined $3,000. Employers therefore must collect pertinent (though private) information about each worker *and provide it to the IRS as well.*

5. No one knows why the law discriminates against businesses with fifty or more employees. But it does. A fast food chain with forty-nine uninsured employees could be hit with a $40,000 fine for adding that fiftieth worker (50 - 30 = 20 x $2,000). Dan Danner of the National Federation of Independent Businesses explained "the law's employer mandate effectively tells small businesses, 'Do not hire more than 49 employees.'"[4]
6. Employers who opt not to provide the mandated coverage will see their labor costs go up about 98 cents an hour. That's the $2,000 fine spread out over the 2,200 hours the average employee works. That's compared to the $1.79 an hour to provide the government-mandated plan.

A Mandate That Actually Reduces Coverage

One of the major goals of Obamacare is to increase the number of people with health insurance, but the employer mandate actually makes employers less likely to offer it. The Congressional Budget Office forecasts that fewer people will get coverage on the job after the law goes into effect than if the law had not passed. Only the "Washington knows best" crowd could concoct a health law that makes it harder for you to keep your health plan and your job.

It's a matter of arithmetic. Provide a long list of "essential benefits" OR pay a $2,000 per worker fine. The fine is a bargain compared with the price tag of the "essential benefits."

Deloitte Consulting estimates that 10 percent of employers will drop coverage.[5] Lockton Benefit Group reports that 19 percent of their mid-size business clients are planning on dropping coverage, while the McKinsey survey of employers who already know what the new law says reports that 50 percent or more are planning to stop offering insurance.[6] The Urban Institute argues that employers will still offer coverage to compete for the best workers, but in the current job market that argument is unconvincing.[7]

Employers won't balk at providing the expensive mandated health plan to a $500,000-a-year heart surgeon or a

$250,000-a-year stockbroker. But the mandate could price a young, unskilled job seeker out of the market.

If you work as a waitress, receptionist, sales clerk, or fast food chef, or in another modest-paying job, you may have to say good-bye to health insurance—and just hope your job doesn't disappear as well. Chili's Grill and Bar chain, which has almost 1,300 restaurants nationwide, is looking to eliminate busboys when the new health law goes into effect.[8]

Hiring a Minimum Wage Worker Will Be Costly, but Hiring a Minimum Wage Worker with a Family Will Be Prohibitive

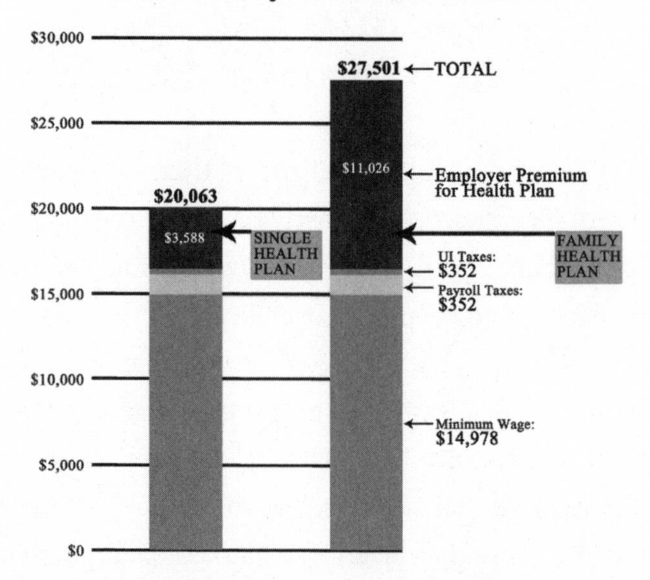

Source: James Sherk's "Minimum Yearly Costs Incurred by Employers per Full-Time Employee, Based on 2,000 hours of work." Calculations based on data from the US Dept. of Labor, Congressional Budget Office estimates of premiums in 2016 under PPACA and the 2010 Medical Expenditure Panel Survey—Insurance Component. Oct. 11, 2011

Employers can't offset the new health insurance cost by cutting pay for minimum wage workers. There is no place to cut; the law won't allow it. Employers are left with these options:

1. Don't offer insurance and pay the federal fines.
2. Replace full-time workers with part-time workers.
3. Replace workers with automated teller machines and automated check-outs.

So here's what we can expect as the employer mandate goes into effect. Look for more part-time jobs ahead. Young, inexperienced workers who, before Obamacare, could have landed a full-time starter job may be forced to juggle part-time jobs and enroll in Medicaid. The Congressional Budget Office estimates that about one half a percent of the workforce—or about 700,000 people—will stop working full time and go on Medicaid as a result of the new law.[9] FactCheck.org, a left-leaning arbiter of the truth, says that's a "small net job loss." It's not small, if it's your job.

Meanwhile, mid-size companies with slim profit margins will be affected most by the mandate. Grandy Payne came to Washington, D.C., to warn the politicians how the added cost of health insurance will drive him out of business. Payne's company makes wooden crates at eleven plants in Texas, Oklahoma, Mississippi, Tennessee, Georgia, Florida, South Carolina, and Virginia.

Only about half of his employees currently get insurance at work, because the other half don't feel that contributing to health insurance is a good way for them to spend their pay. But under the Obama health law, he will have to enroll them, find out how much their husbands and wives make, and set the employee contribution at a level deemed "affordable." He says it will be an "administrative nightmare."

His other option is to stop insuring his workers and pay the $2,000-per-worker fine, which will amount to $1 million a year. That's more than the company's annual profit. Payne told the politicians that his company is caught in "no-man's land" between the small businesses that don't have to provide insurance and the big companies and unions that somehow manage to get waivers.[10]

Waivers from the Employer Mandate?

What about those waivers? The brief history of Obamacare waivers suggests that certain companies and unions may not have to comply with the employer mandate, while others—who don't have a Washington lobbyist or an inside track to the White House—will.

When the early provision of the Obama health law barring mini-med plans went into effect, employers with large numbers of low-paid retail and restaurant workers protested immediately. They made it clear: exempt us from this law or we will drop coverage altogether.

Nothing in the law empowered the Obama administration to exempt anyone, but the Secretary of Health and Human Services handed out waivers to certain companies and certain unions.

Will companies and unions be granted waivers from the employer mandate when it takes effect in 2014? Nothing in the wording of the legislation gives the Obama administration the authority to do that either, but the letter of the law didn't deter the president last time.

What about Coverage for Your Spouse and Children?

The Obama health law's ambiguous wording left the issue of family coverage in limbo. Ever since the law was enacted, there has been a legal battle raging over whether employers have to cover only their employees or also their employees' dependents. The letter of the law says that employers can ask their workers to contribute up to 9.5 percent of their household income for an individual plan, but it says nothing about limiting what the worker contributes for family coverage. The IRS so far says employers are off the hook. They don't have to pay for family coverage, period.

The bottom line is that some workers who get family coverage on their job now may get only individual coverage after the mandate goes into effect in January 2014. Oops, just the opposite of expanding coverage! But family coverage as defined by Obamacare costs a huge amount, and many employers will balk at paying the tab for the family of an entry-level worker. It could add more than $5 an hour to the cost of hiring a waiter or sales clerk, for example.[11]

So the Obama administration will have to sort out what happens to families who lose coverage when the mandate goes into effect. Will they be eligible for Medicaid or a plan on the state insurance exchanges? It remains to be seen.

CHAPTER SEVEN

THE HEALTH INSURANCE EXCHANGE—IT'S NOT LIKE SHOPPING AT THE MALL

Did you know?

- Using a state insurance "exchange" will mean shopping for insurance online or going to a government office similar to the DMV
- Only Americans under thirty can meet the mandate requirement to buy insurance by purchasing a "catastrophic" health plan
- You can choose "Bronze," "Silver," "Gold," and "Platinum" plans, but the only difference between them is the size of your co-pays and deductibles, not levels of quality

You've probably never heard of a health exchange, but you may be shopping on one in 2014. That's when you'll have to prove to the IRS that you have an insurance plan with "essential benefits," as the government defines them. If you are under age sixty-five, earn too much to qualify for Medicaid, and no longer get coverage through an employer, get ready to shop on the exchange.

Section 1311 of the health care law says that each state "shall establish an American Health Benefit Exchange." Many states are in a fury over what they perceive as the federal government commandeering state employees and state resources to do the federal government's bidding. As of November 2012, nearly half the states were still refusing to set up exchanges. "I'm not lifting a finger," Maine's Governor Paul LePage said. "We're going to let Mr. Obama do a federal exchange. It's his bill," LePage said. He added that "a state exchange puts the burden onto the states and the expense onto our taxpayers, without giving the state the authority and flexibility" it needs.[1] Ohio Governor John Kasich, Louisiana Governor Bobby Jindal, and Wisconsin's Scott Walker echoed that conviction.

The Obama health law says that if any state fails to set up an exchange meeting federal standards by 2013, the federal government will come into the state and do it. Though the governors who refuse to set up exchanges won't be able to stop the federal government from coming in, their refusal could save their states' taxpayers some money. And here's an added glitch. The law clearly omitted any reference to a federally established exchange handing out subsidies to health plan buyers. So it may be that in states that refuse to set up exchanges and let the federal government do it, subsidies won't be available. Stay tuned, and thank the politicians for the chaos.

In the meantime, get ready to shop on the exchange if you are currently uninsured or an employer drops your coverage. While the politicians argue, you may have to comply with the new mandate for health insurance.

Shoppers on the exchanges will log on to a government-sponsored website and purchase a plan. There will also be toll free numbers and government offices (like the DMV), in case you don't want to use the Internet. Less populous states may set up regional exchanges with neighboring states.

The One-Size-Fits-All Plan

On the exchange, you'll see brands such as Blue Cross or WellCare, all offering the same essential benefit package. You can choose from the Bronze, Silver, Gold, and Platinum versions. If only we were talking about jewelry! But far from precious metals, these are simply different levels of cost sharing. Bronze plans cover 60 percent of your medical costs, whereas Silver covers 70 percent, Gold covers 80 percent, and Platinum covers 90 percent. Of course you pay more up front to get Platinum, and then have lower co-pays and deductibles when you seek medical care.

You've heard President Obama pledge many times that under the new law, insurers would have to compete "based on quality and cost," and consumers wouldn't have to worry about differences in what is covered or what the fine print says. Like comparing apples to apples. It sounds good. But keep in mind, it also means only having one choice—apples.

Imagine the federal government telling car makers, "no more hatchbacks or convertibles, offer only four-door sedans so consumers won't get confused."

Another difference between a health exchange and the mall is that at the mall, you have to pay your own bill. On the exchanges, a large portion of the shoppers will be getting taxpayer-funded subsidies to help pay for their insurance. In a way, the exchange is like the health welfare store.

Here is what you need to know: your subsidy (if you can get one in your state) will be based on your household income. The subsidies will reduce the premium you actually have to pay, because taxpayers are picking up the rest of the tab. If you qualify for a subsidy, you will also have lower deductibles and out-of-pocket costs than someone else buying the same plan without using a subsidy.

Who Can Use the Exchange? How Much Do You Have to Pay?

Anyone who doesn't get health insurance through Medicare, Medicaid, or an employer is eligible to shop on an exchange. Legal immigrants are not eligible for Medicaid during their first five years in the United States, but surprisingly they can shop on the exchanges and receive subsidies with no waiting period. Illegal immigrants are barred from the exchanges and free of the mandate. They are expected to get their care at federally-funded community health centers.[2]

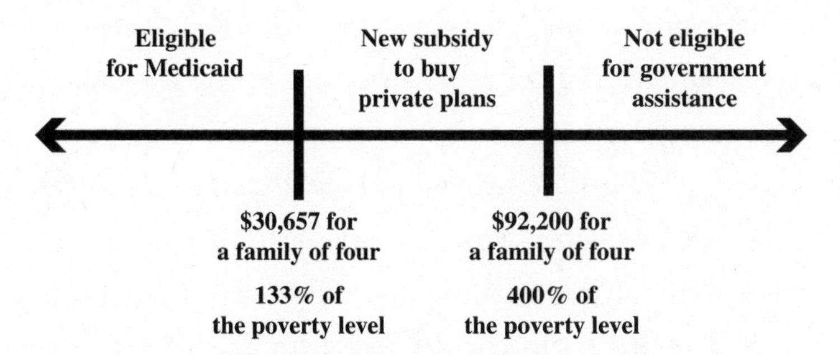

Even if your employer offers health coverage, you can shop on the exchange if you think the plan offered at work would require you to pay more from your paycheck than you can afford. If you do enroll on the exchange, though, your employer may have to pay a $3,000 penalty for failing to offer you "affordable" coverage.

If you're under thirty and don't think you'll need much health care, the government allows you to meet the individual mandate requirement by purchasing a "catastrophic plan." The name is a bit misleading. Catastrophic health insurance generally means the kind almost everyone had two generations ago. It covered the large, unexpected costs that occur when you have an accident or get rushed to the hospital with a serious illness. This "catastrophic" option, open only to the young, also includes preventive care and three visits to your primary care doctor per year.

No matter what your age, you'll be compelled to enroll in a plan and pay what the government says you can afford. The health insurance exchange is one place to do that.

Some people see a similarity between the Obamacare state insurance exchanges and the Massachusetts Health Connector. You can take a look yourself at www.mahealthconnector.org. The new Obamacare exchanges are definitely different from the Utah insurance exchange, the only other insurance exchange in the country. In Utah, the exchange offers a wide range of products, and free market forces determine the prices and what consumers buy. Under Obamacare, the government makes the decisions.

SHOP: The Small Business Health Insurance Options Program

Beginning in 2014, small businesses (up to one hundred employees) may buy coverage on a special exchange in each state called SHOP—the Small Business Health Insurance Options Program. Starting in 2017, states will have a choice to open SHOP to larger employers. The rationale for keeping it small at the outset is that larger employers tend to have older employees who would push up premiums. The idea behind SHOP is to give small businesses purchasing clout they would lack on their own. Unlike the small business tax credits, which expire in 2016, the SHOP feature of Obamacare is intended to be permanent.

CHAPTER EIGHT

MEDICAID NATION

Did you know?

- Expanding Medicaid is the chief way that the law covers the previously uninsured
- Surgery patients with Medicaid face a higher risk of dying than patients with no insurance at all
- Expanding Medicaid raises premiums for people with private insurance

Expanding Medicaid is the key component of Obamacare. Even after the June 2012 United States Supreme Court ruling giving states the option of *not* expanding Medicaid, this expansion is still the way most currently uninsured people will gain coverage. The new law transforms Medicaid from a temporary safety net to a permanent entitlement in place of private insurance.

All states have Medicaid, though some give it a distinctive name such as TennCare in Tennessee and Medi-Cal in California. Medicaid was created in 1965, and CHIP (the Children's Health Insurance Program) was added to it in 1997. Ever since 1965 the federal government has set minimum standards but otherwise given states leeway to determine eligibility and benefits based on what state taxpayers wanted and state budgets could handle. Federal taxpayers paid half the cost in some states and a bit more in others. Even so, Medicaid has become the biggest item in many states' budgets and the second biggest in the rest.

Fast forward to 2014. The Obama health law urges states to open up Medicaid to many more people and pledges to pay all or nearly all the cost (90 to 100 percent) for those newly eligible.

New Medicaid Rules in Some States

States that go along with the new federal rules will open up Medicaid to residents with incomes up to 133 percent of the poverty level (roughly $33,000 for a family of four in 2014). States adopting the federal rules will also open Medicaid to childless adults, not just pregnant women and families, and disregard an applicant's assets when determining eligibility. People with limited incomes would be eligible, no matter how much money they have in the bank or what else they may own.[1]

Some States Will Not Expand Medicaid

These changes alone would cause a 57 percent increase in Medicaid enrollment in Texas, a 49 percent increase in Oklahoma, a 42 percent increase in Florida, a 41 percent increase in Virginia, and similarly huge enrollment increases in nearly a dozen other states.[2] For that reason, several governors, including Texas governor Rick Perry, have announced that their states will not go along with the Medicaid expansion.

Many states will go along, looking at the federal promise of funding as a pot of gold. But a report of the nonpartisan State Budget Crisis Task Force, released July 17, 2012, and chaired by two big-time Democrats—former lieutenant governor of New York Richard Ravitch and former Federal Reserve chairman Paul Volcker—warned that Medicaid expansion could push states into financial crisis if the federal government breaks its promise to fully fund it. That could be a punishing blow to anyone who pays state taxes.

Will the federal government go back on its word? It wouldn't be the first time government broke a promise. Though the Obama health law says the federal government will pay the tab for expanding Medicaid, any future Congress can undo that commitment. If that happens, state taxpayers will be left holding the bag, just when state budgets (and taxpayers) are already strained to the breaking point.

If You're a Taxpayer

Of course whether it's the states paying or the federal government paying, it's really YOU the taxpayer paying. Under the Obama health law, Medicaid becomes the fastest-growing part of the nation's health care spending, outpacing Medicare—despite the aging of the baby boomers.

If You Lose Coverage at Work and Wind Up on Medicaid

In addition to newly eligibles, an unknown number of low-income workers who have private insurance are expected to lose it and be dumped into Medicaid, according to government actuaries. If you are a waitress, sales clerk, or entry-level job holder, that could be you. I use the term "dumped" because seldom do people with private health insurance volunteer to switch to Medicaid. But when the new mandates on employers start in 2014, many businesses will say covering employees is too expensive with the "Washington knows best" mandates and stop doing it. Your boss could be one of them. If you're in a relatively low-paying job, your next stop may be Medicaid.

Health care advocates are already warning of the unintended consequences of the huge increase in Medicaid enrollment for truly poor Americans. It's already very difficult to find doctors willing to take Medicaid. The dean and CEO of Johns Hopkins Medicine, Edward Miller, warned that the expansion of Medicaid enrollment could have "catastrophic effects" at places like Hopkins.[3]

Sadly, Medicaid care is often inferior care. University of Virginia researchers reviewed the experiences of nearly 900,000 patients undergoing eight different surgical procedures. Shockingly they found that Medicaid patients were 50 percent more likely to die in the hospital after surgery than patients with private coverage. Even more amazing, according to the *Annals of Internal Medicine*, Medicaid patients were 13 percent more likely to die than patients with no insurance at all.[4] Researchers also found that Medicaid patients who undergo angioplasty to open up clogged arteries are twice as apt to have another heart attack or other serious circulatory problems as patients with private insurance.[5]

What the research shows is that Medicaid patients get worse care—but, ironically, not cheaper care. The inferior care they get results in more complications, and the complications lead to longer hospital stays and higher costs. It's only reasonable to question whether expanding Medicaid is a good idea when patients already on Medicaid are getting dangerous care at high costs.

Heart patients on Medicaid are less likely to receive angioplasty when they need it, and asthmatic children on Medicaid don't see specialists. In fact, few specialists in any field take Medicaid.[6] When people with heart disease on Medicaid can't see a cardiologist, expanding the Medicaid program and worsening the shortage of specialists could be deadly. No wonder health advocates are concerned.

If you're likely to be on Medicaid in 2014, these are important issues to know about. The fact is, doctors either don't take Medicaid or limit how many Medicaid patients they will see because Medicaid shortchanges them.

Medicaid Shortchanges Doctors, Patients, and Taxpayers

Medicaid pays on average about 86 cents to 91 cents for every $1 of care delivered. It shortchanges hospitals and doctors. To make ends meet, doctors and hospitals have to charge privately insured patients more. That pushes up your premium. The well known health care consultancy Milliman & Robertson estimates that short-changing by government programs forces families with private insurance to pay at least $1,500 a year more in added premiums.That's *before* the new Medicaid expansion. These experts caution that once Obamacare's vast Medicaid expansion occurs, private premiums will be pushed even higher.[7]

The Obama health law offers only a band-aid solution. It increases what Medicaid pays primary care doctors—but only for a year!

Medicaid Expansion Will Push Up Private Premiums

The more Medicaid is expanded, the higher private premiums will go. As a taxpayer, you pay for Medicaid three times—first when you pay your federal taxes, then when you pay your state taxes, and a third time when you pay your own insurance bill.

CHAPTER NINE

THE ALTERED HEALTH INSURANCE LANDSCAPE

Did you know?

- Under Obamacare, fewer Americans will get health insurance through an employer than if the law had not passed
- Entry-level employees who lose insurance at work will get "dumped" into Medicaid
- When Obamacare is fully implemented, the federal government will pay for half of the health care Americans use

When Obamacare is fully in effect, the health insurance landscape will be transformed. The federal government will pay for an amazing 49.9 percent of all health care in America. Half! The new federal entitlements will not just cover those who were previously uninsured. They will also cover millions of people who were self-sufficient until Obamacare offered to pay for their health insurance—or pushed them out of private insurance into government programs.

Despite the employer mandate, fewer people will be getting insurance through a job than if the law had not passed. Some employers will say the mandate costs too much and settle for paying fines instead.

Some of the people who were insured on the job will be forced into the insurance exchanges, and others will find themselves "dumped" onto Medicaid, alongside the vast majority of those who were uninsured before the law went into effect.

The increase in government dependency, some say, could change the character of America. By 2019, families earning over $100,000 a year will be eligible for federal subsidies. And millions of Americans will be permanently on Medicaid, which used to be a temporary helping hand or safety net for the poor.

CHAPTER TEN

MORE BENEFITS (EVEN ONES YOU DON'T WANT) = HIGHER PREMIUMS

Did you know?

- "Free" preventive care is not free. You pay for it up front in your premium
- The Obamacare law expands the services insurers *must* cover and you *must* pay for. That will raise your premium
- Covering children up to age twenty-six on their parent's plan raises *your* premium even if you don't have adult children

There is no tooth fairy. The more your health plan covers and pays for, the more it's going to cost. Obamacare imposes an expensive array of new mandates on the insurance industry. That means, ultimately, it's imposing higher premiums on you.

"Free Preventive Care"

Section 2713 of the law, which went into effect in September 2010, prohibits co-pays for preventive services.

The president has boasted that the new health law provides "free" preventive care, but it's not free. It's prepaid. The law forces you to pay for a mammogram, a Pap smear, and a colonoscopy up front, when you pay your premium, whether you intend to get the tests or not. If you do get the test, there will be no deductible or co-pay. But clearly the test isn't free.

Being forced to pay up front for a colonoscopy feels almost as bad as having to get one.

There are several other provisions, called "consumer protections" in the law, that are already driving up premiums.

No Annual or Lifetime Caps on Benefits

As of September 2010, insurance companies can no longer put a lifetime cap on what they will pay out to cover your medical costs. This requirement applies even to the small number of "grandfathered plans" that survive under Obamacare.

The new law also phases out annual caps on payouts. Annual caps must be raised to at least $2 million in September 2012 and eliminated in January 2014.

It sounds wonderful, but it also means you can no longer have the option of being covered by one of those mini-med plans commonly offered to entry-level workers in many industries.

In fact, no sooner was this new provision put into effect than the White House was inundated with complaints from some of the biggest employers in America. They said that they couldn't afford to provide comprehensive insurance for low-wage hourly workers.

The White House responded by granting a total of 1,472 waivers to certain companies and unions, exempting them from the law. But in 2014 those waivers will run out. If you currently have a mini-med plan at work, be aware that you're likely to lose coverage in 2014.

Children Can Be Insured on Their Parent's Plan to Age Twenty-Six

This is another whopper of a premium hiker. Many parents and their adult children like this idea, and with or without Obamacare, this provision could have gotten through Congress. The provision took effect September 2010, and it applies to adult children. (But parents on Medicare and certain retirement plans cannot add their adult children.) Of course, this new provision benefits some families at the expense of others. If you don't have adult children, you are paying a higher premium for your family plan to keep your neighbor's adult child covered.

More Premium Hikes to Come

The biggest premium hikes are ahead. Even before Congress passed Obamacare, the Congressional Budget Office warned that individual and small group premiums would cost more under the law than if the law had not been passed. In other words, members of Congress voted for Obamacare knowing it would raise your insurance costs. A major reason is the one-size-fits-all benefit package.

"Essential Health Benefits" Covered

This provision, which kicks in on January 1, 2014, will mean that every health plan sold to you on the exchanges or provided through an employer will have to be packed with benefits—all costing something—for you to meet the legal requirement that you have "qualified" health insurance. You have to pay for in-patient substance abuse treatment coverage even if you have no intention of ever taking drugs, for example.

It's like passing a law that the only car you can buy is a fully loaded Cadillac.

No Rejections for Pre-Existing Conditions

No other feature of the Obama health law has gotten more attention than the provision, which goes into effect in 2014, prohibiting insurance companies from denying coverage to people with pre-existing conditions. Often this is the one-liner used to justify the entire 2,572-page law.

People with hypertension, diabetes, and other pre-existing conditions should be able to get health insurance. But the fact is, most already can.

Less than one percent of the U.S. population has been denied coverage for a pre-existing condition, according to federal Health and Human Services data.[1] Even before Obamacare, no one with a pre-existing condition could be barred from employer-provided coverage (the way most people are insured), or from Medicare and Medicaid.

Denials came only in the small individual market (serving just 5 percent of the population). Even there, four out of five people with pre-existing conditions had no difficulty getting coverage, according to HHS data.

Pre-existing conditions simply do not constitute a major problem, in terms of the numbers of people affected. But you know the drill for politicians. Create a crisis and then purport to solve it.

The Obama health care law set up a temporary federal high-risk pool for applicants with pre-existing conditions. It's been a flop. Only 86,000 people with medical conditions gained coverage, according to NCSL data.[2] That's 86,000 out of a population of over 300 million—less than .00023 percent of the people in the United States. Hardly enough to justify overhauling the health care system. Surely there must be some less costly way—less costly not just in dollars spent, but also in deleterious effects on our health care system and on millions of Americans' health—to meet the genuine needs of this tiny minority?

In most states, people with pre-existing conditions are already getting help through a subsidized high-risk pool. That's the right approach, and far better than what New York and New Jersey have done. These two states require insurers to sell policies to healthy people and sick people at the same price. The result is the highest premiums in the country, because healthy people drop out to avoid paying the high premiums—which of course, pushes premiums even higher.

Obamacare follows the New York/New Jersey approach but makes buying insurance mandatory. How many young healthy people will go along with that, rather than forking over the penalty? Economists disagree. The jury is still out.

Medicaid Expansion Also Boosts Premiums

There is no disagreement, however, about the impact of the expansion of Medicaid in 2014. Premiums will skyrocket.

Medicaid underpays doctors and hospitals, and they have to make up for it by charging privately insured patients more. The average household with private insurance pays at least $1,500 a year extra to their insurer because of Medicaid. The higher Medicaid enrollment goes, the higher private premiums will go, too. Private premiums are estimated by the Medicare actuaries to rise an astounding 7.1 percent in 2014, the year the mandated benefits and Medicaid expansion go into effect.[3]

CHAPTER ELEVEN

RAIDING MEDICARE— HOW SENIORS WILL PAY FOR OBAMACARE

Did you know?

- The Obama health law awards bonus points to hospitals that spend the least on seniors
- Hospitals will be whacked with demerits for care that seniors consume up to thirty days after leaving the hospital, including physical therapy
- Doctors will be paid less to treat seniors than any other patients, even less than patients with Medicaid

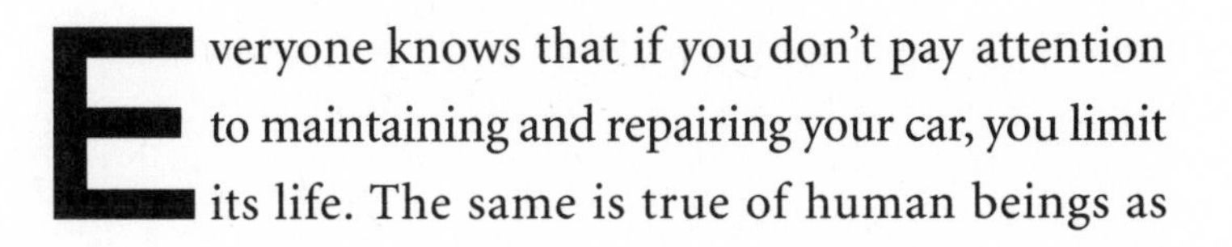

Everyone knows that if you don't pay attention to maintaining and repairing your car, you limit its life. The same is true of human beings as they age. We need medical care to avoid becoming clunkers—worn out, parked in wheelchairs or nursing homes.

For nearly half a century, Medicare has enabled seniors to get that care. But the Obama health law removes over half a trillion dollars in future funding from Medicare over the next decade. The new law:

- Slashes what doctors, hospitals, homecare agencies, hospice care, and dialysis centers are paid to care for the elderly,
- Penalizes hospitals for providing generous care, and
- Cuts support from Medicare Advantage plans.

These cuts are being made just when 30 percent more people will be entering Medicare, as baby boomers turn sixty-five. The numbers do not add up. Baby boomers who are counting on Medicare will get less care than seniors currently get. Data from the Obama administration's own actuaries indicate that Medicare will spend $1,431 less per senior in 2019 than if the law hadn't passed.[1]

Paying for the New Entitlements: Seniors Pay the Lion's Share

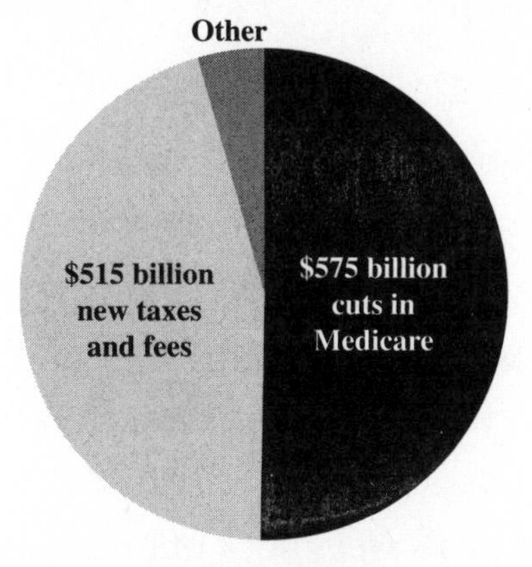

Some people refer to $575 billion in Medicare cuts and others say $716 billion in cuts. Both figures are accurate. It depends on when you start counting. The cuts total $575 billion over a decade if you begin counting in 2010, and $716 billion over a decade if you begin counting in 2012. The cuts get larger as the years go on.

Source: CMS, April 22, 2010; CBO, July 2012

Across-the-Board Payment Cuts

Doctors, hospitals, hospice care, nursing homes, and dialysis centers will be paid substantially less to care for seniors than if the law had not been passed, and in some cases even less than Medicaid pays. The Obama administration's own Chief Actuary of Medicare, Richard S. Foster, bravely warned Congress that the cuts would reduce seniors' ability to get the care they need.[2]

Foster warned that unless these cuts are repealed, about 15 percent of hospitals could stop accepting Medicare. Where will seniors go if their local hospital stops taking Medicare?

Other hospitals will be forced to operate in an environment of scarcity, with as many as 40 percent in the red, according to Foster. That will mean fewer nurses on the floor, fewer cleaners, and longer waits for high-tech diagnostic tests. It will affect all patients.

Obamacare's defenders say that cutting Medicare payments to hospitals will knock out waste and excessive profits. Untrue. Medicare already pays hospitals less than the actual cost of caring for a senior, on average 91 cents for every dollar of care. No profit there. Pushing down the reimbursement rate further, as the Obama health law does, will force hospitals to spread nurses thinner. When Medicare reduced payment rates to hospitals as part of the Balanced Budget Act of 1997, hospitals incurring the largest cuts laid off nurses. Eventually patients at these hospitals had a 6 to 8 percent worse chance of surviving a heart attack and going home, according to a National Bureau of Economic Research report.[3]

Peter Orszag, former Budget Director and Obamacare supporter, ignores this evidence and tries to reassure seniors that Medicare spending could be cut by 30 percent without harming seniors.[4] He cites the *Dartmouth Atlas of Health Care 2008*, which tries to prove that patients who get less care—fewer hospital days, doctors visits, and imaging tests, have the same medical "outcomes" as patients who get more care.[5] But read the fine print.

The Dartmouth authors arrived at their dubious conclusion by studying the records of patients who had already died. Of course the patients treated at the high-spending hospitals and the low-spending hospitals had the same end result. They were all dead!

Fortunately, researchers have set the record straight. Data published in the *Archives of Internal Medicine* show that seniors treated in hospitals providing more intense care and greater spending have a better chance of recovering, going home, and resuming their lives.[6] Seniors treated at the lowest-spending hospitals die needlessly. Researchers found that 13,815 California seniors treated at low-spending hospitals would have survived and left the hospital had they received the extra care provided at higher-spending hospitals. Reducing care at the very end of life may be wise, but these across-the-board Medicare cuts will result in reduced care for all patients, including those who could survive their illnesses and go home if they get the care they need.

New Medicare Efficiency Measures

In addition to the across-the-board cuts in payments to hospitals, Section 3000 of the Obama health law actually awards bonus points to the hospitals that spend *the least* per elderly patient. The bonus system went into effect on October 1, 2012. Hospitals that spend the least "per Medicare beneficiary" get rewarded, and hospitals that spend more get whacked with demerits. This despite the evidence that patients have a better chance of surviving at higher-spending hospitals. Hospitals will even be penalized for care consumed up to thirty days after patients are discharged—for example, for outpatient physical therapy following a hip or knee replacement.

Subjecting Seniors to the Ravages of Aging

Five procedures have virtually transformed the experience of aging for Americans: knee replacements, hip replacements, angioplasty, bypass surgery, and cataract operations. Older people used to languish in nursing homes or be trapped in wheelchairs. Now many can continue to lead active lives. The Obama health law threatens to undo that progress. The across-the-board cuts in hospital payments and the rewards for hospitals that spend the least per senior will make all these procedures harder to get and less safe.

Astoundingly, doctors will be paid less to treat a senior than to treat someone on Medicaid—and only about one-third of what a doctor will be paid to treat a patient with private insurance, according to Chief Actuary Foster. On July 13, 2011, he warned Congress that seniors will have difficulty finding a doctor to treat them. Even doctors who do continue to take Medicare won't want to spend time doing procedures such as knee replacements when the pay is so low. Yet the law bars them from providing the care their patients need for an extra fee. You're trapped.

Some people seem to think too many seniors are getting these procedures. At a town hall debate in 2009, President Obama told a woman, "Maybe you're better off not having the surgery, but taking the painkiller."[7]

Science proves that attitude is wrong. Knee replacements, for example, not only relieve pain but also save lives. Seniors with severe osteoarthritis who opt for a knee replacement are less apt to succumb to heart failure and have a 50 percent higher chance of being alive five years later than arthritic seniors who don't undergo the procedure, according to the *Journal of the American Medical Association* research.[8]

When assessing what the impact of Medicare cuts will be on you and your family, ignore the political rhetoric and look at the scientific evidence. The cuts will doom seniors to more painful aging and shorter lives.

Dr. Seymour Cohen, an oncologist named to "America's Top Doctors," summarized the dire consequences during a physicians' forum on the health law: "When we went to medical school, people used to die at 66, 67, and 68. Medicare paid for two or three years. Social Security paid for two or three years. We're the bad guys. We're responsible for keeping people alive to 85. So we're now going to try to change health care because people are living too long. It just doesn't make very good sense to me."[9]

Prevention

Section 4104(a) of the new law expressly authorizes the Secretary of Health and Human Services to reduce preventive services for seniors based on the recommendations of the U.S. Preventive Services Task Force. (That's the panel that recently caused public outrage by saying women ages forty to forty-nine and older than seventy-four should no longer get routine annual mammograms.) A half-page later, the law empowers the Secretary to "increase" preventive services for Medicaid recipients. The winners and losers here could not be clearer.

The law says,

> SEC. 4105(a). Evidence-Based Coverage of Preventative Services in Medicare.
> (n) Authority to Modify or Eliminate Coverage of Certain Preventative Services.—Notwithstanding any other provision of this title, effective beginning on January 1, 2010, if the Secretary determines appropriate, the Secretary may—
> (I) modify—
> (A) the coverage of any preventative service described in subparagraph (A) of section 1861 (ddd)(3) to the extent that such modification is consistent with the recommendations of the United States Preventative Service Task Force....

Advantage Plans

Nearly one out of every four seniors is in a private Medicare Advantage plan, rather than traditional Medicare. Medicare Advantage was launched in 2003 to give seniors the option of choosing a private health plan with the government paying most of the cost. These plans cost the government (and thus taxpayers) about 10 percent more, but they also provide seniors with more benefits. They are hugely popular because of extras such as vision and dental care—and occasionally even gym memberships—that traditional Medicare doesn't cover.

Medicare Advantage is singled out for big funding cuts under the Obama health law. Medicare Advantage funding will be slashed by 27 percent—meaning $3,700 less per year for each senior enrolled by 2017. The result is that plans will offer fewer extras, and many plans are expected to go out of business entirely. Medicare actuaries predict that enrollment will plummet to half what it would be without Obamacare.[10] The president promised, "If you like your health care plan, you'll be able to keep your health care plan, period."[11] But that's definitely not true for the 7.4 million seniors expected to lose the choice of Medicare Advantage.

The Independent Payment Advisory Board

Over and above the half trillion in cuts to future Medicare funding, Section 3405 of the Obama health law creates a fifteen-member board of unelected cost-cutters called the Independent Payment Advisory Board (IPAB). It's meant to be "independent" of the public and shielded from the wrath of senior voters.

The IPAB's job is to identify further cuts in what doctors, hospitals, hospice care and other providers are paid to care for seniors. IPAB can't cut benefits, we're told. But those are weasel words. IPAB can push the payment for a hip replacement lower and lower, until it is so low that medical professionals can no longer afford to provide that treatment. Even the Congressional Budget Office has warned that as the nation's debt crisis worsens, Medicare benefits will be put on the IPAB chopping block.

IPAB is a radical departure from Medicare as we've known it. In creating IPAB, Congress cedes nearly all control over Medicare spending to unelected bureaucrats. Congress is admitting it doesn't want to make unpopular cuts and then face seniors. The Obama health law says that whatever cuts IPAB "recommends" automatically go into effect *unless* Congress enacts a different set of Medicare changes with the same net savings. That arrangement—making IPAB into a lawmaking body—turns the U.S. Constitution on its head, many argue.

Already IPAB has aroused opposition all across the political spectrum, even from supporters of the Obama health law, such as former Representative Pete Stark (California Democrat) and the AARP. Perhaps anticipating the opposition, the law's drafters included a provision laughable in its brazen defiance of the U.S. Constitution.

This provision states that IPAB can be repealed only in a tiny window of time. The repeal must be submitted to Congress between January 1 and February 1, 2017 (not sooner or later) and enacted by August 15 of that year. In reality, no Congress can bind any future Congress. IPAB can be repealed any time the people's elected representatives choose to repeal it, and many will say the sooner the better.

Saving Medicare

You've probably heard the claim that the cuts in future Medicare spending will secure the program's financial future. That claim is even repeated in Medicare's mailings to seniors. But the truth is, Medicare is being raided, not saved. The funds taken from Medicare are not set aside to extend the program's solvency. Instead they are spent on new entitlements for people under sixty-five. Chief Actuary of Medicare Richard Foster and Director of the Congressional Budget Office Douglas Elmendorf candidly told Congress that Medicare cuts would not prolong the life of the program. To claim otherwise would be cooking the books.[12]

Closing the Donut Hole: "Let Them Eat Cake"

Politicians have talked much less about the cuts to future Medicare funding than about the sweeteners. The most publicized is "closing the donut hole," which means gradually adding Medicare Part D drug coverage for seniors who use between $2,800 and $6,400 worth of prescriptions a year.

Previously, Medicare Part D paid for most medication expenses up to the $2,800 mark, but then seniors who needed more drugs had to pay 100 percent of the cost until their purchases reached a whopping $6,400 a year. For the small number of seniors with costly chronic illnesses, the donut hole was a big problem. The new law gradually fills in this coverage gap with money provided partly by the federal government (taxpayers) and partly by rebates sent directly to consumers by pharmaceutical companies. If you've ever fallen into the donut hole, your Medicare Part D drug plan will tell you how to get help in the future.

But don't be misled. The cuts in Medicare funding are ten times as large as the sweeteners.[13]

CHAPTER TWELVE

OBAMACARE'S NEW TAXES—HOW THEY MAY AFFECT YOU

Did you know?

- Your ability to deduct medical expenses will be reduced starting in 2013
- Your tax-free contributions to a Flexible Savings Account will also be limited starting in 2013
- Generous "Cadillac" health plans will be taxed at 40 percent starting in 2018

There is no question that seniors bear the biggest cost of Obamacare. But taxpayers also pay for it. There are twenty new taxes or tax hikes in the law. It's "the largest set of tax law changes in twenty years," according to Treasury Inspector General J. Russell George.[1] The IRS says it will need more than a thousand new auditors and $359 million in 2012 alone to administer the new health law.[2]

Medicare and Payroll Tax Hikes, Plus New Taxes on Tanning Salons and Home Sales

One of the biggest sources of new tax revenue will be a hike in the Medicare hospital insurance tax—though the extra revenue will *not* be going to Medicare. Currently, the tax amounts to 2.9 percent of your gross pay, with employer and employee each paying in 1.45 percent. The new law raises the employee portion to 2.35 percent for high earners (with no hike in the employer contribution). Individuals who earn more than $200,000 a year and couples who make more than $250,000 per year are considered high earners; they will pay the higher rate starting in 2013.

Increased Medicare Hospital Insurance Tax (2013 & After) for Couples Earning More than $250,000 a Year

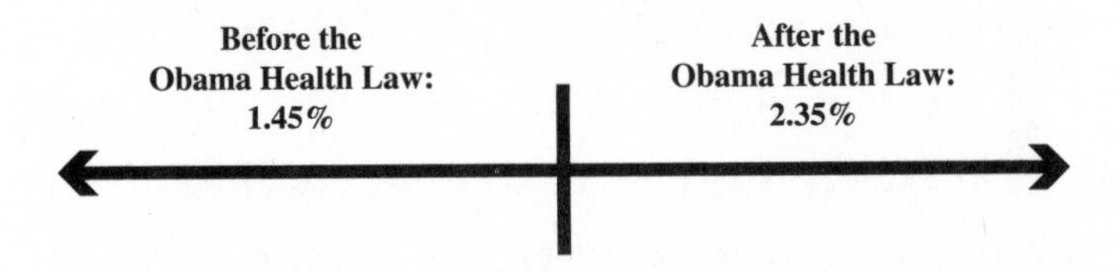

The even bigger change will be a new 3.8 percent Medicare tax on "unearned income," meaning gains from stocks, bonds, dividends, rents, vacation homes, and even, under some circumstances, the sale of your primary residence. (Once again, the name is misleading because the revenue will not go to Medicare.) A person with modest income could become a "high earner" and be hit with that 3.8 percent tax if he sells his home and makes a large profit. This tax applies *in addition to capital gains taxes.* Note: people who sell their primary residence get a once-in-a-lifetime $500,000 exclusion.

New Medicare Investment Income Tax (2013 & After) for Couples Earning More than $250,000 a Year

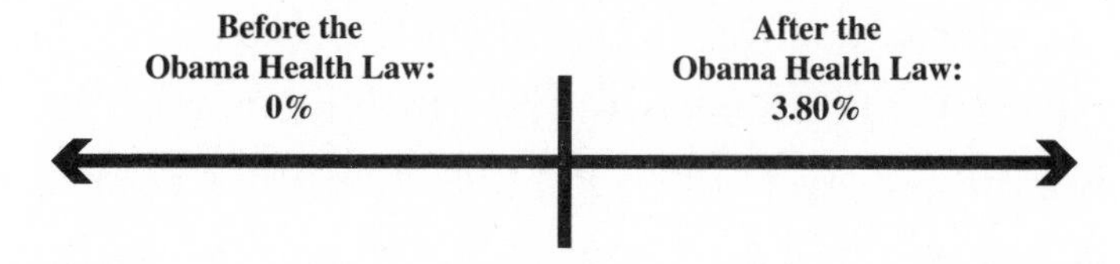

Obamacare also imposes a new 10 percent tax on indoor tanning services, which must be paid either by the tanning salon or the customer. This new tax is expected to raise about $1.5 billion in revenue over the next decade.[3]

New Taxes on Pharmaceuticals, Medical Devices, and Health Insurance Companies

Even if you're neither a high earner nor a tanning salon customer, you'll be affected by the new Obama taxes.

Several taxes, totaling an estimated $107 billion over the law's first decade, will technically hit insurers, medical device companies, and pharmaceutical companies, but you can assume the costs will be passed on to you, the consumer, in the form of higher prices.

The new health law slaps a tax on all health insurers, based on the number of premiums they collect. This tax will hit small businesses, their employees, and people who pay for their own individual policies. One of the goals of health reform was to make coverage more affordable. But this tax will do just the opposite. The Joint Committee and the CBO confirm that this tax will be passed on to consumers and raise their premiums, costing the average family $300 to $400 dollars a year in added premium costs. A troubling 87 percent of small business owners will be hurt by this tax.[4] Unlike big companies that self-insure, small business owners buy policies for their workforce and will ultimately pay this premium tax.

Other taxes nominally on the health care industry include a tax on the manufacture or importation of medical devices, which will likely raise the cost of hip and knee replacements, and taxes on brand name pharmaceuticals.

Aside from the indirect impact of these taxes on the industry, other changes in the tax rules may affect you.

Higher Penalty on Health Savings Account Disbursements

Do you have a Health Savings Account? The new law doubles the IRS penalty from 10 percent to 20 percent for non-allowable purchases made using funds in Health Savings Accounts or Flexible Savings Accounts.

Starting in 2011, funds in these accounts may be used only to buy prescription drugs, not over-the-counter drugs. If you want to buy Tylenol or Advil with these funds, you'll need to get a prescription first.

New Limits on FSAs

Do you have a Flexible Savings Account? Beginning in 2013, employees will be able to make tax-free contributions of only $2,500 a year, down from the unlimited amount in the past. Overall, the new law is stacked against you paying for your health care out of pocket or on your own, rather than with insurance.

Fewer Medical Deductions

Do you usually deduct medical expenses when you do your taxes? Up to now, you could deduct expenses that exceeded 7.5 percent of your income. Beginning in 2013, you'll lose the medical expenses deduction unless your expenses exceed 10 percent of your income. (For seniors, however, the change comes in 2017, not 2013.)

Penalties against Employers and Individuals

Another revenue source is what employers and individuals will be forced to pay if they are caught without government-prescribed health insurance. By 2022, the CBO estimates that these penalties will amount to $172 billion.[5]

Excise Tax on "Cadillac" Health Insurance

Finally, beginning in 2018, a "Cadillac" tax on health plans that cost more than $16,300 for an individual or $27,500 for a family is scheduled to go into effect. The tax is a whopping 40 percent, imposed on the insurer who sells the plan—but of course, it will be passed on to the consumer. It is a major source of payment for the Obamacare entitlements, providing $111 billion by 2022—the second biggest revenue producer among the twenty new taxes in the law.

Despite the tax's nickname, "Cadillac" health plans are held by a much broader range of people than Wall Street tycoons and other one percenters. Many union workers have them. In fact, the tax was originally supposed to take effect much sooner, but powerful unions pushed Congress to both delay its effect and exclude many union workers in "high-risk" occupations. Longshoremen even got the law amended after it was passed, to expressly identify their occupation as high risk and immune from the tax.

So will the Cadillac tax ever take effect? It's impossible to say. It's hard to imagine that a future president and Congress will have more fortitude than the law's namesake has to impose it.

Obamacare and the Deficit

Defenders of the Obama health law cite claims by the Congressional Budget Office that repealing the health law would increase the deficit. Repeal would cancel $890 billion in new entitlements, said the CBO, but also eliminate revenues of greater magnitude.[6]

Don't be bamboozled by the CBO's budgetary gymnastics. Just because Obamacare—in theory—raises more money than it spends is hardly reason to keep it, or any law.

The Obama health law creates two costly give-aways—an expansion of Medicaid and subsidies for private health plan purchasers—and pays for them by hiking taxes and raiding funds previously designated for Medicare. The tax hikes and reductions in funds to care for the elderly (each over half a trillion dollars) together total more than the entitlements during the next ten years, says the CBO, and produce a small $109 billion surplus. Repealing the law would erase that tiny surplus. So what! Repeal would reduce government spending, lower taxes, and undo the evisceration of Medicare; all good things.

Recently published projections from the Centers for Medicare & Medicaid Services (CMS) fill in the grim picture of what Obamacare will do to the nation, and correct dangerous misconceptions voiced by some of the nation's top politicians who responded to the CBO report.

Senate Majority Leader Harry Reid (Nevada Democrat) has said the CBO report "confirms what we've been saying all along: the Affordable Care Act saves lots of money."[7] Untrue. CMS data show cumulative health spending over the next decade will be $478 billion higher than if the law had not been passed. Health care spending as a share of Gross Domestic Product will rise from 17.9 percent in 2010 to 19.6 percent in 2021, and government (and ultimately the taxpayers) will be paying for a larger share of it than ever before.[8]

House Democratic Whip Steny Hoyer (Maryland) has said that the CBO "makes it very clear: the Affordable Care Act is controlling the growth of healthcare costs."[9] Also untrue. Health care spending was growing at the slowest rate in many decades when Obamacare was passed, inching up only 3.9 percent in 2009 and again in 2010. But CMS predicts spending will shoot up 7.4 percent in 2014, when Obamacare goes into full effect.

In worse news, private insurance premiums will increase 7.1 percent that year, says CMS, which is 4.1 percentage points higher than if the health law had not been passed.

The only area of health care spending that will grow more slowly is Medicare, because of the cuts made by Obamacare and further cuts under the Budget Control Act of 2011. Seniors are bearing the brunt in every budget deal made by the Obama administration.

Don't be misled by the CBO's fuzzy math and Washington's infatuation with deficit reduction.

In Washington today, "deficit reduction" is code for increasing taxes faster than spending. It means freedom reduction. If we're really interested in cutting the deficit, we need entitlement reform to reduce spending. And the best way to start is by repealing the two new entitlements in the Obama health law before they go into effect.

CHAPTER THIRTEEN

PHYSICIANS DIAGNOSE OBAMACARE

Did you know?

- The American Medical Association (AMA) lost members in 2010 and 2011 because it supported Obamacare
- The Obama health law gives the Secretary of Health and Human Services oversight over doctors' decisions, even for patients with private health plans they paid for themselves.
- Many doctors are considering leaving the medical profession

Aside from seniors, the group most opposed to the Obama health law is doctors. Of course, they want their patients to have access to affordable health care—the nominal purpose of the law.

But many doctors oppose the law because it will drown them in red tape and paperwork, reduce their earnings, and empower government bureaucrats to interfere in how they care for patients.

The American Medical Association

Physician opposition to the Affordable Care Act undoubtedly surprises many people because the American Medical Association (AMA) endorsed the law. But only about 17 percent of practicing doctors belonged to the AMA at the time, and AMA membership dropped in 2010 and 2011 because of the organization's support for Obamacare.[1] Doctors see Obamacare as a threat to their livelihood—and more.

"Doctors Going Broke"

That was a CNN headline on January 5, 2012.[2] Stingy payments from government programs such as Medicare and Medicaid are largely to blame. On average, a physician paid by Medicare gets only 81 percent of what a private insurer pays for the same care.

Medicaid rates are even worse, on average only 56 percent of what private insurers pay.[3] The new health law clobbers physicians' livelihoods in two ways—by vastly expanding Medicaid enrollments and severely cutting payment rates for patients on Medicare.

There's more to physician discontent than just dollars and cents, however. Doctors are "drowning in Alphabet Soup," as Dr. Hal Scherz puts it. Scherz is founder and president of Docs4PatientCare. He calls the Obama health law a "compliance nightmare," and cites the huge number of reporting requirements that will turn doctors into paper pushers instead of healers.[4]

Beginning in 2015, doctors who don't submit a long list of health measurements on their patients will be penalized by losing 1.5 percent of their Medicare reimbursements—a serious matter since Medicare already shortchanges physicians. Measuring quality is important, but who is going to do all the paperwork?

Worse than these hurdles of paperwork and inadequate payment rates, what doctors object to most is the government's interference in how they care for patients. When Medicare and Medicaid were established nearly a half-century ago, the law said that the federal government could not interfere with treatment decisions. Over the decades, some of that protection was whittled away. Now the Obama health law puts government directly in charge.

Controlling Medical Decisions

In fact, the framework for this top-down control was actually slipped into the "stimulus" legislation, or American Recovery and Reinvestment Act, passed in February 2009. One provision called for doctors and hospitals to install and use electronic health information technology. Beginning in 2014, Medicare and other federal programs will impose financial penalties on doctors and hospitals that are not "meaningful users" of the technology.

What is "meaningful use"? Electronic health records can help make sure that if you're injured and rushed to the emergency room, your records—including, for example, the information that you are allergic to penicillin—will reach the hospital ahead of you, even if you are thousands of miles from home. This technology has the potential to save lives and money. Unfortunately, "meaningful use" means a lot more than that. Doctors already see the signs that the technology will put "Washington knows best" bureaucrats in charge at the bedside—using computers to tell doctors what to do.

Dr. David Blumenthal, the first appointee to head President Obama's Office of the National Coordinator for Health Information Technology, said at the outset that his job was not about "just putting machinery in offices." It's about control. Blumenthal predicted "many physicians and hospitals may rebel—petitioning Congress to change the law or just resigning themselves to . . . penalties."[5]

How much leeway will doctors have to order the tests and treatments they think are needed? It's hard to say, because the stimulus legislation empowered the government to make the standard of "meaningful use" more "stringent" over time.

The Obama health law extends control of doctors beyond what they do for patients in government programs. For the first time in history, this law empowers the federal government to dictate how doctors treat privately insured patients—patients who aren't on Medicaid or Medicare but instead have private insurance from companies such as Aetna or Cigna. Even if you pay your own premium, the government is still in charge. For many health care advocates as well as physicians, this is the most important issue of all: the transfer of decision-making authority from the doctor at your bedside to the federal government.

Section 1311 (h)(1) of the Obama health law states that you have to be in a "qualified plan," and qualified plans can pay only doctors who follow the dictates of the federal government. The new law says that the Secretary of Health and Human Services—appointed by the president—can impose any regulation to "improve health care quality." That can literally cover *everything in medicine*, from whether you get a hip replacement to what tests your doctor orders to follow up on equivocal mammogram results.

The controls on doctors embedded in the Obama health law have made some physicians pessimistic about the future of their profession and even disheartened enough to quit practicing. Americans are already facing a doctor shortage. The profession's gloomy assessment of the new law's impact on their finances, their job satisfaction, and the future quality of medicine will likely worsen that shortage.

CHAPTER FOURTEEN

CONSTITUTIONAL SHOWDOWN AHEAD

Did you know?

- There are many legal challenges to Obamacare ahead—it's a full-employment project for lawyers
- The Supreme Court has already ruled that the federal government must not "define general standards of medical practice in every locality." And that's what the Obama health law does
- The HHS mandate that Catholic institutions cover contraception for their employees may be struck down by a federal court

Just minutes after President Obama signed the Patient Protection and Affordable Care Act into law on March 23, 2010, the state of Florida filed a lawsuit challenging its constitutionality. Virginia also sued, challenging the mandate. All in all, twenty-eight states have challenged Obamacare. On June 28, 2012, the high court ruled that Congress can compel Americans to buy insurance. That ruling opened the way for implementation of nearly every aspect of the law.

But there is more courtroom drama ahead. Americans of every political persuasion, from far left to far right, are challenging specific provisions of the law. At stake is your medical privacy, your doctor's ability to make decisions for you, and your freedom to practice your religious beliefs.

Can the Federal Government Standardize Medical Care?

Can the federal government dictate how doctors treat privately insured patients? In all likelihood, this provision (Section 1311 of the law) will be challenged by the pro-privacy high court.

Consider how the court ruled in *Gonzalez v. Oregon* (2006). Oregon had passed a Death with Dignity Act allowing lethal drugs to terminally ill patients who requested them. The Bush administration argued that assisted suicide was not "legitimate" medical care, and therefore federal agents could halt the use of the drugs under federal drug enforcement laws. The Supreme Court ruled 6–3 against the Bush administration's interference. Such intrusion, the Court said, "would affect a radical shift of authority from the States to the Federal Government to define general standards of medical practice in every locality." That's exactly what the Obama health law does.

Before the current Obamacare debate, the public discussed government interference in medical decisions largely in one context: abortion. When a lower federal court struck down the Partial Birth Abortion Ban Act in 2004 (a decision later reversed by the Supreme Court), Planned Parenthood President Gloria Feldt said, "This ruling is a critical step toward ensuring that women and doctors—not politicians—can make private, personal health care decisions."[1] During the litigation, federal authorities requested access to medical records to determine whether partial-birth-abortion procedures were ever medically necessary. Privacy advocates defeated every request.

The Obama health law raises the same medical privacy issues in a broader context than abortion. The mandate for electronic medical records creates a "tell-all" relationship with every doctor you see. See a psychiatrist? Your foot doctor will know about it. So will many non-physicians who have access to the data. The National Committee on Vital and Health Statistics, a federal advisory committee, proposed permitting patients to carve out categories of information, such as mental or reproductive health, from their records. The Goldwater Institute, a free market think tank suing to overturn the law, argues that the law violates privacy rights by compelling Americans to share "with millions of strangers who are not physicians confidential private and personal medical history information they do not wish to share."[2] There is no doubt these privacy concerns will have their day in court.

Freedom of Religion

The Bill of Rights makes protection of religion its first priority. Its framers put religion right at the top, in the

First Amendment. Government is barred from "prohibiting the free exercise" of religion. But the Obama administration is testing that prohibition, requiring Catholic institutions to provide their employees with health plans that cover sterilization, birth control, and even a "morning after" drug.

The teachings of the Catholic religion prohibit contraception, sterilization, and abortifacient drugs—anything that makes procreation impossible.

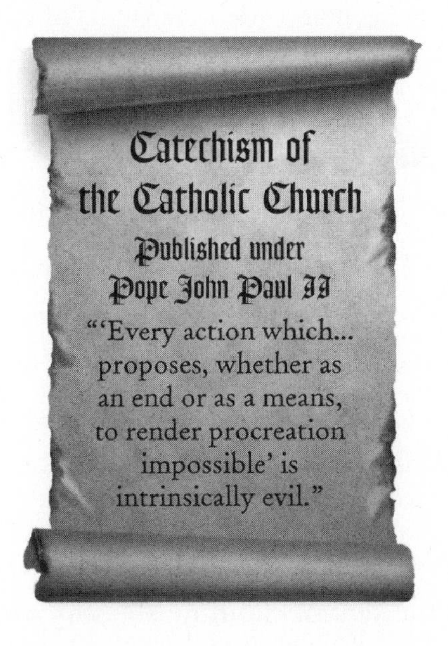

The Obama administration has refused to exempt religious institutions that serve the public at large—meaning both Catholics and non-Catholics—from this mandate. Catholic schools, Catholic charities, and Catholic hospitals are all coerced by the sweeping mandate that requires employers to provide insurance for contraception and sterilization. Catholic organizations that *serve only Catholics* are exempt, but most Catholic institutions regard it as their mission to help all in need, not just people of their own faith.

The Amish are exempt from carrying any insurance under the Obama health law. The law also recognizes the tenets of the Christian Scientists and respects them. Quakers have long been accorded the rights of conscientious objectors to war. Catholic leaders such as Archbishop Timothy Dolan are asking, why are Catholics not given the same respect?

The outcome of this constitutional battle could hinge on another freedom of religion case decided by the Supreme Court just weeks before the battle over the contraception mandate hit the front pages, *Hosanna Tabor Evangelical Lutheran Church v. Equal Employment Opportunity Commission*. Here's the interesting story of *Hosanna Tabor.*

Cheryl Perich, a teacher at a Lutheran school in Michigan, sued the school claiming she was wrongly fired because of a disability, narcolepsy, which made her sleepy all the time. The school said she was fired for pursuing litigation, against the teachings of the Lutheran Church, instead of resolving the dispute in a Christian way with her community. The high court ruled on January 8, 2012, that a church has the freedom, under the First Amendment, to set its own standards for those who are part of its ministry. The federal government cannot interfere, said the court, affirming a "ministerial exception" to federal employment law.[3]

In the *Hosanna* case, the Obama administration's solicitor general argued that churches and church schools are no different from other private associations. They have to obey federal law. But Chief Justice John Roberts wrote that the Obama administration's position is "hard to square with the test of the First Amendment itself, which gives special solicitude to the rights of religious organizations."

If federal courts interpret the *Hosanna* precedent narrowly, Catholic churches will be exempt from purchasing insurance that includes contraception, but Catholic hospitals that treat non-Catholics will not. But if the breadth of the First Amendment and the *Hosanna* decision are brought to bear, the mandate will be ruled unenforceable on all those whose beliefs it violates.

That means not only Catholic institutions but also businesses owned and operated by people whose Christian views conflict with abortion and contraception. In October, 2012, the Weingartz Supply Company secured temporary relief in a Michigan federal court, and Hercules

Industries won relief in a Colorado federal court. These cases all challenge the Obama administration's narrow view of the First Amendment—that it guarantees only freedom to worship, not freedom to practice religious teachings in everyday life, including at work.

The Independent Payment Advisory Board

The Independent Payment Advisory Board is "independent in the worse sense of the word," Diane Cohen of the legal think tank the Goldwater Institute told Congress. IPAB is "independent of the will of the people."[4]

The Obama health law says that IPAB's czars "recommend" what doctors and institutions are paid. But that is slippery language. IPAB's recommendations automatically become law unless Congress passes—with a three-fifth's supermajority in the Senate—a medical spending plan achieving the same "savings."

These IPAB czars make laws affecting our health care unless Congress enacts legislation to accomplish the same end. The people's *elected* representatives are not even given the option of rejecting altogether the Medicare cuts and determining that cutting Medicare by that amount would be too severe and harmful.

The Supreme Court has not looked favorably on such exemptions from popular oversight. For example, in the high court's 2010 ruling in *Free Enterprise Fund v. Public Company Accounting Oversight Board*, the justices ruled that a board created to administer Sarbanes-Oxley had too much independence. The Constitution does not permit Congress, which has to face the people on election day, to delegate its responsibilities to unelected boards and councils.

Members of Congress swear to uphold the Constitution, but they routinely enact laws without giving the Constitution a moment's taught. Many are ignorant of what it says. They should be required to take a course.

CHAPTER FIFTEEN

DECODING WHAT WASHINGTON SAYS ABOUT HEALTH "REFORM"

Did you know?

- At the time Obamacare was passed, health care spending was increasing more slowly than at any time in the last century
- The Obama health law is already causing premiums to go up
- Obamacare's emphasis on preventing sickness rather than treating it will shortchange the seriously ill

The 2,572-page Obama health law is packed with thousands of inscrutable passages. This guide is designed to decode them. But to make wise decisions about Obamacare, you also need to translate the claims made by Washington politicians about health care.

One misconception in particular can be dangerous to your wallet. Four others are dangerous to your health. Here they are, straight from the mouths of Washington experts and parroted day after day by the media.

1. "Skyrocketing costs" are making it impossible for families to afford health insurance. Without health reform, soaring health costs will destroy our economy. These doomsday warnings, which were instrumental in the passage of Obamacare, were simply untrue. At the time, health care spending was increasing more slowly than at any time in the last half century. Spending increased 10.3 percent in 1970 and 13 percent in 1980, but only 3.9 percent in 2009 and 3.8 percent in 2010.

National Health Expenditure Annual Growth from Previous Year (1970–2014)

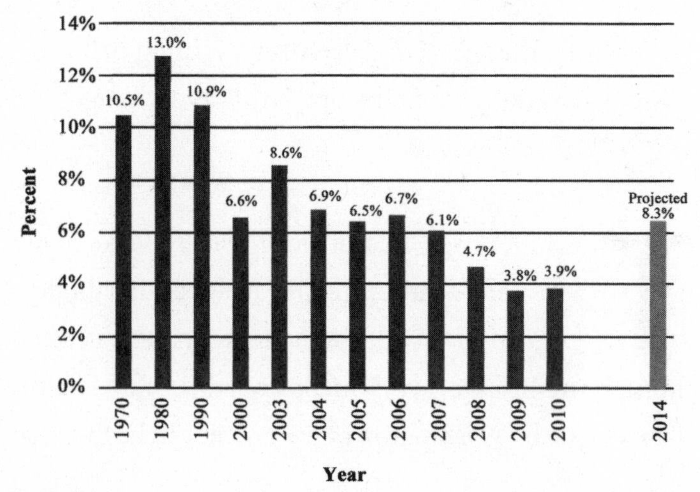

Source: CMS

Sadly the changes imposed by the new Obama health law will force up health care spending and premiums. The actuaries at the Centers for Medicare & Medicaid Services predict that spending will shoot up to 19.8 percent of GDP by 2020, up from 16.6 percent before the health law was passed.[1]

Worse still, premiums are already soaring and will continue to rise. Now that government requires you to buy a health plan packed full of government-mandated "essential benefits," it is going to cost more.

The Obama health law continues a pernicious trend, started in many states, to require health insurance plans to cover more and more. Since 1975, the share of health care Americans pay for out of their own pockets, rather than through insurance, has steadily declined, all the while causing premiums to rise *faster* than health costs.

Share of Personal Health Care Expenditures Paid Out of Pocket

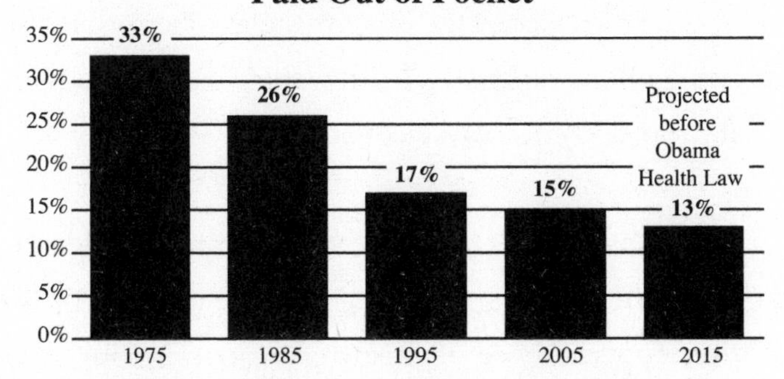

Out-of-Pocket Spending Declining Even before the Obama Health Law

Source: Congressional Budget Office

New York is a case study of bad insurance policy made by venal lawmakers in exchange for campaign contributions from lobbyists. Over the years, lobbyists for chiropractors, acupuncturists, mental health professionals, wig makers, and others rewarded the legislature for passing laws requiring that every health plan cover all these services—fifty-one requirements in all. Each mandate may add just half a percent to the cost of insurance, but that totals a 25 percent premium increase. As I've said before, it's like passing a law that the only car you can buy is a fully loaded Cadillac sedan.

There's a better way. New Jersey saw health plan enrollment dropping, so the state let insurers offer pared-down plans. Sales boomed. New Jersey, with half the population of New York, has three times as many privately insured residents, notes health policy expert Tarren Bragdon of the Empire Center for Policy Research.[2]

This lesson was lost on the "Washington knows best" experts. They repeated the exact mistake New York made, insisting on an expensive "comprehensive" health plan. That means no choices for consumers.

2. "We have to get to a system of keeping people well, rather than treating sickness," said the director of the White House Office of Health Reform, Nancy-Ann DeParle, on March 23, 2009.[3] That would make sense if all disease were behavior-related, but many cancers and other diseases are linked to genetics or unknown causes. DeParle's pronouncement echoes how Sir Michael Rawlins, a British health official, explained his nation's low cancer survival rate. The British National Health Service, he said, has to be fair to all patients, "not just the patients with macular degeneration or breast cancer or renal cancer. If we spend a lot of money on a few patients, we have less money to spend on everyone else. We are not trying to be unkind or cruel. We are trying to look after everybody."[4]

This approach—spreading the care thinly and widely—is deadly for those people with serious illness. In the U.S., about 5 percent of the populace needs 50 percent of the care according to the federal Agency for Healthcare Research and Quality.[5] Health care needs are very skewed. The drumbeat heard in Washington, D.C., to shift resources from treatment to prevention should worry any family dealing with Alzheimer's, Parkinson's, cerebral palsy, or a history of cancer.

3. The U.S. needs to slow the development and diffusion of new medical technology. Imagine any industry or nation thriving on such a philosophy. Yet that misconception is driving "reform" in Washington, D.C. Dr. Ezekiel Emanuel, one of the most influential advisors on the legislation, criticized Americans for being enamored with technology.[6]

New technology accounts for more spending increases than any other factor, even the aging of the population. But a 2008 report from the Congressional Budget Office reminded us that these innovations "permit the treatment of previously untreatable conditions."[7]

Walk into an electronics store, and you will see an array of products that didn't exist a year earlier. The same is true if you go into the hospital. Treatments for heart disease and strokes are as unlike care in the 1980s as flat-screen televisions are unlike the early black-and-white sets.

If you had a heart attack in the 1980s and made it to the hospital alive, you still had only a 60 percent chance of surviving until the end of the year. Now your chance is over 90 percent.[8]

Overall health spending easily could be reduced by settling for the standard of care and symptom relief available to patients in previous decades, warns the CBO. But there is no demand for 1980s medicine, at 1980s prices, and in ten years no one will want 2012 medicine at today's prices, either.

4. "The only way to slow Medicare spending is to slow overall health system spending through comprehensive and carefully crafted legislation," declared Secretary of Health and Human Services Kathleen Sebelius.[9]

Forcing Americans to settle for a lower standard of medical care in order to save Medicare is akin to forcing all Americans to go on diets and buy fewer groceries because the food stamp program is running out of money.

Medicare can be fixed without putting the nation on a regimen of medical scarcity with fewer nurses in the hospital, less access to technology, and pressures on doctors to do less. The safe alternative is to reduce the government's share of the cost of health care, rather than reducing the nation's overall standard of care. That can be accomplished by inching up the eligibility age for Medicare and asking wealthy seniors to pay more.

But the Obama health law moves the nation in the opposite direction. According to CMS projections—the administration's own projections—government will pay 50 percent of health care costs by 2020.

Once the Obama health law enrolls millions more people in its new entitlements, how will it limit demand and control spending? The answer is by lowering the standard of care for everyone and compelling Americans who already had insurance to do with less. That is why the new health law imposes so many controls on your doctor and your insurer.

5. Americans should settle for Europe's standard of medical care. On June 1, 2009, the president's Council of Economic Advisors issued a report pointing to Europe's skimpier health care consumption and urging Americans to copy it.[10] But the truth is, 90 percent of the difference in per capita health care spending is due to higher incomes in the U.S. Greater wealth, not more waste, is the cause.[11] Americans earn more so they spend more.

Unfortunately, many of the key architects of the Obama health law were admirers of Europe's scarcity model. David Blumenthal, for example, National Coordinator for Health Information Technology from 2009 to 2011, extolled the advantages of top-down government controls to limit consumption.[12]

Members of Congress and other Washington elites are misled by bogus claims that the U.S. spends the most for health care and gets little for it.

Former Senator Tom Daschle, an early spokesman for President Obama's health reform plans, told *Meet the Press* in August 2009 that Americans were spending too much and getting poor-quality health care. "The World Health Organization listed us 37th just below Costa Rica and above Slovenia," he said.[13]

Mainstream media outlets bought into that preposterous ranking and disseminated it far and wide. It was repeated on CNN's *Larry King Live*,[14] and the *Tampa Bay Times* even cited it to rebut Senator John McCain's claim that the U.S. has the best health care system in the world.[15]

Anyone who cared about the truth would have looked into how the WHO arrived at its thirty-seventh-place ranking for the United States. WHO ranked the U.S. number one on the only measure that counts: "Responsiveness to the needs of the patient." But on other measures, such as "Financial fairness" and "Health distribution," WHO gave the high marks to countries where the government pays for all health care and where equality reigns—with all patients receiving equally poor care.[16] What mattered to the WHO rankers were socialism and other ideological priorities—not whether a patient gets needed treatment to survive cancer.

The truth about the WHO ranking came out on April 22, 2010, one month after the Obama health law was signed. Dr. Philip Musgrove, editor in chief of the WHO Report, announced in the *New England Journal of Medicine*, that it was "long past time for this zombie number [37] to disappear from circulation." He added that "there are sound reasons to mistrust the conceptual framework behind the estimates."[17]

Thank you, Dr. Musgrove, but it's a bit late.

The stakes are high and they are not political. All Americans want the best health care for their families. Right now, if you are seriously ill, the best place to be is in the United States. A man diagnosed with prostate cancer has a 99 percent chance of surviving it in the U.S. It is not a death sentence here. But in Europe, nearly one out of every four men diagnosed with prostate cancer dies from it.[18]

And if someone in your family has what is currently considered an "incurable" illness, America is still the nation of hope. This is where the cures are developed. Since 1950, scientists working in the United States have won more Nobel Prizes in medicine and physiology than the entire rest of the world combined.

Nobel Prize Winners in Physiology or Medicine by Country before Passage of Obamacare

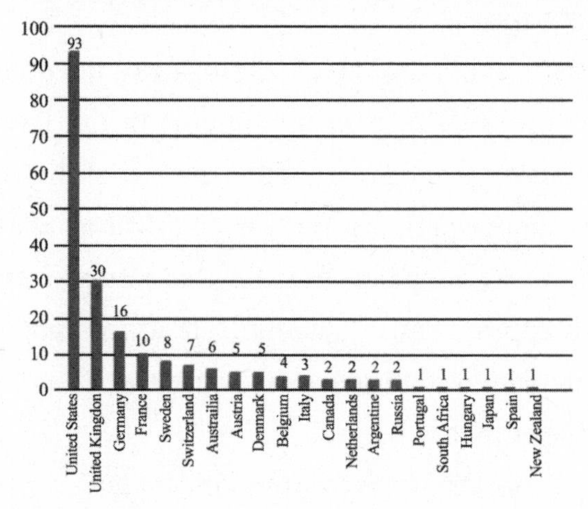

This chart shows Nobel Prize Winners in Physiology or Medicine ranked by country. The Nobel Prize Winners in Physiology or Medicine has been awarded to 196 Nobel Laureates between 1901 and 2010.

CONCLUSION

The Obama health law pursues a worthy goal: expanding health insurance coverage to those who cannot afford it. But the law's consequences—unintended by many of its supporters—will lower your quality of care, put government in charge of your care, and bring down the curtain on the golden age of medicine.

A half century ago, it was not uncommon for Americans to die in their fifties or early sixties from heart disease. My own father did. At that time, heart disease killed 1.7 million Americans every year. Now, according to the National Institutes of Health, the death rate is less than a quarter of that.[1] Physicians at bedside and researchers in labs have achieved an amazing leap in longevity for most Americans—seven years of added life. And those additional years are high-quality years. Disability among the elderly has plummeted, and older people travel, play sports, and enjoy grandchildren instead of languishing in wheel chairs and nursing homes. Unfortunately this remarkable progress, fueled by costly technology and the ingenuity and dedication of physicians, is threatened by the government controls imposed by the Obama health law.

Obamacare redistributes health resources *from* Medicare recipients—seniors and baby boomers—and *from* people who pay for their own private health plans, in order to vastly expand Medicaid coverage for the uninsured. The tax hikes in the Obama health law pay for far less than half the actual cost of covering the uninsured. Most of the resources come from limiting the care received by those who already have insurance. Limiting care requires government controls on the decisions of your doctors.

To make this monumental shift of decision-making authority from the doctor at your bedside to the federal government palatable, the president and the supporters of his health law have engaged in a systematic and shocking campaign to vilify doctors.

At a White House press conference on July 22, 2009, President Barack Obama said "Right now doctors a lot of times are forced to make decisions based on the fee payment schedule that's out there. So if they're looking—and you come in and you've got a bad sore throat, or your child has a bad sore throat or has repeated sore throats, the doctor may look at the reimbursement system and say to himself, you know what, I make a lot more if I take this kid's tonsils out. Now that may be the right thing to do, but I'd rather have that doctor making those decisions just based on whether you really need your kid's tonsils out...."[2]

That outrageous misrepresentation of what pediatricians do was not an aberration—a mistake made by the president in a tired moment. He said something similar on August 11, 2009, to a crowd in Portsmouth, New Hampshire, this time accusing surgeons of amputating the feet of diabetics needlessly to collect a $30,000 or $40,000 fee.[3] (In fact, Medicare pays surgeons between $740 and $1,140 each for leg amputations, including follow-up care.)[4]

It was a feat of demagoguery, but even more remarkable is the fact that the president got away with it. Though most Americans would still tell you they trust their doctor more than any politician, the president's health plan is now the law.

You and your doctors are going to be making your way through a minefield of new regulations, taxes, and government oversight. I hope you have found the information in the fifteen chapters above helpful. Below is an Obamacare Glossary, which offers additional clarifications to help you survive Obamacare.

THE OBAMACARE GLOSSARY ANSWERS YOUR QUESTIONS

Abortion: The Obama health law says that federally subsidized health plans can offer abortion coverage, but must set up separate accounts to segregate federal funds from money used for abortions. Before the law was enacted, Congressman Joe Pitts (Pennsylvania Republican) and Congressman Bart Stupak (Michigan Democrat) called segregating funds "an accounting gimmick" and proposed an amendment to ban abortions in all federally subsidized health plans.

The Senate majority resisted the amendment, and the president succeeded in getting the health law passed without it. He offered instead an Executive Order reaffirming the Hyde Amendment, a 1976 provision named after the late Representative Henry Hyde (Illinois Republican) that bans federal funds for abortions except in the cases of rape and incest, and to protect the life of the mother.

An Executive Order depends on the whim of the president, and can be changed at any time, pro-life forces argue. In October 2011, pro-life lawmakers tried again for a statute to bar a health plan from offering abortion coverage if any enrollees receive federal subsidies. It passed the House 251–172 but was not taken up in the Senate. In conclusion, whether abortions are funded through federal programs such as community health centers will depend on the discretion of the president and the Secretary of Health and Human Services. The law does not address the issue.

Accountable Care Organizations: On December 19, 2011, Secretary of Health and Human Services Kathleen Sebelius unveiled the first thirty-two Accountable Care Organizations or ACOs designed to reduce Medicare costs. ACOs are groups of doctors and other health care providers, usually including a hospital, that agree to coordinate how they treat a patient with the goal of reducing costs. Coordination might mean shortening hospital stays, for example. Each ACO will treat five thousand or more Medicare patients. If the ACO reduces costs, each caregiver gets a bonus from the federal government. The less it costs to care for a senior, the more doctors and hospitals earn.

American Indians: Attached to the Obamacare legislation is a reauthorization of the Indian Health Care Improvement

Act, which was first passed in 1976 and last reauthorized in 2000. The Obama health law makes it permanent, and expands services to American Indians, including Alaskan tribes and urban Indians. The expansion includes more mental and behavioral health services and dialysis.

Annual Caps: Starting in 2014, the health law bans annual limits on what your insurance plan will pay out when you need care. In the meantime, the law bans limits lower than $2 million.

Automatic Enrollment: Employers with more than two hundred full-time workers must automatically enroll their employees into health plans. Employees can opt out, but employers have no choice.

Baby Boomers: America's 77 million residents born from 1946, when soldiers returned home from World War II, through 1964.

Breast Cancer in Young Women Initiative: Section 399NN of the law directs the Centers for Disease Control and Prevention to create an educational campaign focused on breast cancer awareness in women ages fifteen to forty-four and directs the National Institutes of Health to develop new screening tests to detect breast cancer in young women. Widespread screening by current methods is impractical, it is said, because so few younger women contract breast cancer. Only about 10 percent of the approximately 250,000 women diagnosed each year with breast cancer are younger than forty-five, according to the American Cancer Society. Therefore a different approach is needed to identify those young women at risk of the disease.

Cadillac Tax: In 2018, if you are enrolled in a plan costing at least $16,300 a year ($27,500 for family coverage), your insurance company will be taxed 40 percent for selling you that plan. The Cadillac tax is an excise tax on insurers, and it is designed to penalize and discourage some people from having better or more high-end coverage than everybody else. But remember, limits on what you can pay for insurance also limit what is in the pot to take care of you when you're sick. This tax is also a major source of revenue to pay for the health law.

Centers for Medicare & Medicaid Services (CMS): a division of the Department of Health and Human Services.

Community Health Centers: The Obama health law provides $11 billion in additional funding for community health centers. Now that Americans will all have coverage, the centers will serve largely illegal immigrants, according to HHS officials.[1]

Community Living Assistance Services and Supports (CLASS): This program was designed to provide long-term care insurance for people who would need assistance at home. In November 2009, before the Obama health law was enacted, the Congressional Budget Office warned Congress that CLASS would add "tens of billions of dollars" to the federal deficit within thirty years.[2] But in the first ten years, it would collect premiums and have to pay out very little, amassing cash. In other words, it looked "paid for" in the first decade, but would turn into a deficit exploder later. In the fall of 2011, the Secretary of Health and Human Services conceded that it was financially unsustainable and would be mothballed. You won't be hearing much more about the CLASS program, except for demands to repeal it.

Community Transformation Grants: Section 4201 of the health law empowers the Centers for Disease Control and Prevention (CDC) to hand out grants to local organizations that propose to improve the emotional and social wellness of their community, combat environmental hazards, foster healthy living, and reduce health disparities between races. In 2011, the CDC awarded $103 million in community transformation grants, and it continues to make new grants.

In September 2012, $7.9 million was awarded to Community Health Councils, based in Los Angeles, California.

It's a large amount for an organization that claims to have a $2 million annual budget. On September 26, the organization posted a long list of job openings.

Community Health Councils' mission is "to promote social justice" and ensure more health and community resources go to people of color. However, executive director Lark Galloway-Gilliam has led protests for more than a decade under the organization's banner against fracking, for-profit hospitals, and state budget cuts and has partnered with the Natural Resources Defense Council to file lawsuits against oil drilling.

Community Health Councils says part of the $7.9 million will be used to "educate community members on environmental hazards," and 65 percent will be distributed to its community partners. One partner is Los Angeles Community Action Network, which, according to its mission statement, "promotes voter engagement as a means of civic participation" and conducts "one-on-one education in the streets" as well as "monthly teach-ins for downtown residents." Other partners include tenants' rights advocates, anti-fracking and anti-drilling groups, church groups, and one actual health advocacy group, Families in Good Health.[3]

Comparative Effectiveness Research: Even before the enactment of the Obama health law, Congress approved

$1.1 billion in the stimulus law (2009) to create a new government agency called the Federal Coordinating Council for Comparative Effectiveness Research. Fifteen government officials appointed by the president will oversee evaluations of what medications and treatments work best. Almost all medical journal articles already compare effectiveness—which medication or which treatment approach works better. And of course, more research is better than less. But many doctors are concerned that this federal effort at standardization will lead to cookie-cutter guidelines at a time when new discoveries are pointing in the opposite direction—to the advantages of personalized medicine based on the patient's individual genetic make-up. Doctors also worry that the conclusions of the agency will eventually lead to limitations on which treatments are paid for.

Consumer Operated and Oriented Plans (CO-OPS): Section 1322 of the Obama health law creates Consumer Operated and Oriented Plans, or CO-OPs for short, to compete in each state with for-profit insurers. CO-OPs generally are funded by members, but Obamacare CO-OPs will borrow their start-up funds and reserve balances from the federal government. Administration officials predict that even with "flexible" and "individualized" repayment plans, 40 percent of the loans for start-up costs and 35 percent of the loans for reserves will default, in part because CO-OPs applicants will lack insurance experience, and their proposals will be based on untried models. Week after week leading up to the 2012 presidential election, the administration announced more of these multimillion dollar loans to flimsy start-ups: twenty in all in twenty states, totaling $1.6 billion in government loans, with another $2.2 billion in loans budgeted. It makes the $387 million the government lost to failed energy venture Solyndra look like peanuts.[4]

Cornhusker Kickback: In return for Democratic Senator Ben Nelson's vote in favor of the health care reform legislation proposed by his party, Nelson's home state of Nebraska was promised special treatment that would allow Nebraska taxpayers to avoid paying for "newly eligible" Medicaid enrollees. When news of the deal became public it triggered widespread outrage, with the loudest protests coming from Arnold Schwarzenegger, the only Republican governor to support Obamacare. He demanded that California and every other state in the country get the same deal given to Nebraska. In the end that's what happened.[5]

Cultural Competency Training: Section 5307 of the law requires the Secretary of Health and Human Services to support grants and demonstration projects to promote cultural competency training for nurses and other health professionals.

Dependents: Your household dependents, meaning your children and a non-working spouse, must have health coverage. But your employer does not have to contribute to the cost of that coverage. In what is considered by many to be a drafting error, the authors of the law did not clearly state that dependents are eligible to enroll in coverage on their state insurance exchange when the household breadwinner has individual coverage through an employer but not coverage for dependents. Interested parties have urged the Obama administration to resolve this issue in 2013.

Disparities: In the implementation of the president's health law, the administration is committed to "reduc[ing] differences in the amount and quality of healthcare" that different racial and ethnic groups receive. According to an "Action Plan" written primarily by Assistant Secretary for Health Howard Koh and released by the Obama admistration in 2010, "Although disparities can be viewed through many other lens—for example, socio-economic status, sex, age, level of disability, geography, sexual orientation or gender identity—the Action Plan focuses specifically on race and ethnicity." The Action Plan calls for updating standards for culturally and linguistically appropriate services, training health care interpreters, and developing new software and other technologies to help people with limited English proficiency enroll in Medicaid.[6]

Doctor Shortage: The Association of American Medical Colleges predicts a shortage of 160,000 doctors by 2025. The Physicians Foundation did a survey at the end of 2010 and concluded that the shortage may become even larger as physicians unhappy with the new health law retire early.

Donut Hole: The prescription drug coverage gap in Medicare Part D. Most prescription drug purchases are covered up until a limit, currently $2,800. Then the senior is on the hook for 100 percent of any further drug purchases, until he reaches the catastrophic level of $6,400 in drug purchases in a single year, at which point Medicare Part D pays 95 percent. About one out of four Medicare recipients gets stuck in the donut hole and has to pay the whole cost of some drug purchases. The Obama health law slowly closes the donut hole. (See Chapter 11 above.)

Dual Eligibles: People who qualify for Medicare and Medicaid are called dual eligible. They number approximately ten million, and they are generally the highest-cost patients supported by public insurance. The Obama health law creates a new Federal Coordinated Health Care office within the Department of Health and Human Services to better coordinate their care and control its costs.

Early Retiree Reinsurance Program (ERRP): This provision offered funds to employers who continued to provide health insurance to their early retirees up to age sixty-five. The law said the federal government would reimburse employers for 80 percent of any claim they paid to an early retiree between $15,000 and $90,000. The law allocated $5 billion to fund this reinsurance program. It was intended to run until January 1, 2014, when early retirees could apply for health insurance on the exchanges. But, some would argue, it turned out to be a slush fund for big unions, corporations, and state governments to recoup federal money for obligations they otherwise would have met themselves. The program ran out of money halfway through 2011 and was shut down. Among the largest beneficiaries were California's Public Employee Retirement System, with a $57.8 million claim, and the United Auto Workers, with a $206 million claim.[7]

Emergency Medicaid: This is available to any person whose acute symptoms must be treated, and whose income falls below 133 percent of the federal poverty line, regardless of the person's immigration status.

Emergency Medical Treatment and Active Labor Act: Passed in 1986, this federal law bars hospitals from denying emergency medical care, including childbirth services, to *anyone* who needs care.

Employer Mandate: Any employer with fifty or more full-time employees has to offer insurance that includes what the government deems "essential benefits" or pay a fine based on the number of employees. (See Chapter 6 above.)

Employer Voucher: Employers who can't manage to provide a health plan that is "affordable" for their lower-paid employees, based on what the federal government dictates is the maximum portion of "household income" the employee can pay, can instead offer a voucher that will allow the employee to shop on a state exchange. The voucher shields the employer from a penalty, picks up the cost of the insurance on the exchange, and gives the employee an option. (Employers otherwise have to determine each employee's household income, a tricky question because it requires knowing who else in the family works and what they earn.) See also Free Choice Vouchers below.

Essential Health Care Benefits: Beginning in 2014, everyone must have health insurance that includes "essential health care benefits," as defined by the Secretary of Health and Human Services and state lawmakers.

Exchanges: Section 1311 of the health care law states that each state "shall establish an American Health Benefit Exchange." Generally individuals who do not get on-the-job coverage will be able to go to a website to buy a "qualified" health plan. Section 1321 says if a state fails to set up an exchange meeting federal standards by January 2013, the federal government will come into the state and do it.

Free Choice Vouchers: In addition to the Employer Vouchers discussed above, employees who earn less than four times the federal poverty level and whose share of their premium at work is between 8 percent and 9.5 percent of their household income can choose to enroll in a subsidized health plan on the state exchange instead of getting insurance on the job. If an employee makes that decision, the employer must issue the employee a "free choice voucher" equal to the amount the employer would spend on coverage for the worker's plan.

Health Disparities Data Collection: Section 4302 of the law requires the Secretary of Health and Human Services to ensure that all federally supported health programs collect and report data on race, ethnicity, sex, primary language, and disability status to help reduce disparities in health and health care.

Health Savings Accounts (HSAs): Tax-advantaged accounts available to taxpayers who are enrolled in high-deductible health plans. They began in 2003. If you have an HSA you can contribute part of your income to it, without paying income tax on it, and allow the funds to roll over year to year in the account until you need them to pay for medical expenses. Proponents think HSAs encourage individuals to be more responsible for their health care expenses and more conscious of cost. The Obama health law puts HSAs at a disadvantage, because the new law requires that you pay for all preventive care up front in your premium (rather than from your Health Savings Account when you are actually treated). Also the new health law caps deductibles at $2,000, which is about one third of what is currently allowed. Finally the new health law bars you from using your HSA funds to pay for over-the-counter drugs.

Independent Payment Advisory Board (IPAB): An unelected board empowered to reduce what doctors and hospitals are paid. With the creation of IPAB, Congress has surrendered decisions about Medicare spending to unelected bureaucrats, who are not accountable to the voters. (See Chapter 11 above.)

Medicaid: A government health program for people with low incomes. Medicaid is a means-tested program established in 1965. Until the changes to Medicaid made by Obamacare, the Medicaid program was managed primarily by state governments, which determined eligibility standards and benefits to fit what their own taxpayers and budgets could handle. In 1997, Congress added CHIP, the Children's Health Insurance Program. (See Chapter 8 above.)

Medical Loss Ratio: Health insurers selling plans to individuals and small groups will have to spend 80 percent of premiums collected on medical benefits. Plans sold to large groups will have to spend 85 percent on medical benefits. Plans that fail to meet that rule will have to refund some premium revenue to their enrollees.

Medical Malpractice: Despite urgent demands from physicians, the Obama health law does little to address the high costs of medical malpractice insurance and the costly defensive medicine doctors use to shield themselves from unfair lawsuits. Obamacare awards five-year demonstration grants to states to develop remedies for out-of-control malpractice lawsuits. Critics of this approach would argue that some states, notably Texas, have already proven what works. These states have already developed successful strategies—including caps on non-economic and punitive damages, and special medical courts—that need to be expanded nationwide.

Medical Tax Deductions: Obamacare limits deductions for medical expenses. Through 2012 you can deduct expenses that exceed 7.5 percent of your adjusted gross income. Starting in 2013, that threshold rises to 10 percent.

Medicare: A national health insurance program for seniors and the disabled administered by the federal government. Medicare guarantees access to health care for Americans age sixty-five and older and the disabled of all ages. Medicare has four parts: Part A provides hospital care insurance; Part B covers doctors' visits, home health care, and hospice care. Part D, added by Congress in 2006, provides coverage for medications. Part C, also called Medicare Advantage, allows seniors to participate in private health plans instead of the government-run system. All citizens are eligible, as are legal residents who have been in the U.S. for five years. (See Chapter 11 above.)

Medicare Advantage Plans: Under Medicare Part C, about one quarter of seniors enroll in Medicare Advantage Plans offered by a wide array of private insurers. The Obama health law reduces what the federal government pays to subsidize these plans, and many plans are predicted to cut back on benefits such as vision and dental care and gym memberships—or stop offering coverage to seniors altogether. (See Chapter 11 above.)

Medicare Part A Payroll Tax: Starting in 2013, if you earn more than $200,000 (or you and your spouse earn more than $250,000), your share of the tax will go up from 1.45 percent of your gross income to 2.35 percent. Despite the name of the tax, the additional money does not go to Medicare.

Medicare Tax on "Unearned" Income: Starting in 2013, if you sell your home or another investment and make a profit, or get "unearned income" from dividends, interest, and other sources, you will have to pay a 3.8 percent tax on the gain, in addition to capital gains tax if you are a high earner. A high earner is defined as anyone having an adjusted gross income above $200,000 (or $250,000 for a couple). Warning: you may not earn that much yearly, but if the profit from your home sale, added to your annual income, pushes you into that category, your profit will incur this new 3.8 percent tax. Sales of primary residences may be exempt up to $500,000.

Nutritional Labeling: Section 4206 of the Obama health law requires that all chain restaurants with twenty or more locations, and also vending machine operators, post caloric information next to each food or beverage, including each alcoholic beverage, sold. The requirement will apply even to salad bars, buffet lines, and cafeterias.

Dieters will be grateful, but business owners are complaining about the cost of redoing signs every time they add a new item to their menu. Domino's Pizza estimates this requirement could cost each of its franchisees as much as $4,700 a year.[8]

Observation Care: If you are a senior on Medicare, beware of this. When it is not clear that an ill patient needs to be hospitalized, the patient may not—technically—be actually admitted to the hospital but rather placed under "observation" within the hospital, often in the emergency room. Too often, elderly patients are held "under observation" for two or three days, or more—because the hospital staff are gaming the reimbursement system. The Obama health law penalizes hospitals based on how much they spend on Medicare patients and especially for readmitting them for a second hospital stay. Hospital staff may try to avoid these penalties by keeping an ill senior "under observation." The financial problems for the patients are manifold. "Under observation" doesn't count as hospitalized, so a patient under observation is not eligible for nursing home care when discharged. Also, costs for being "under observation" at a hospital are paid by Medicare Part B instead of Part A, which means larger out-of-pocket costs for the patient. Some Medicare advocacy groups are actually suing to stop the Department of Health and Human Services from allowing "under observation" status.

Parental Coverage: Starting in September, 2010, the law required health plans to cover the "children" of policy holders until age twenty-six.

Part-Time Workers: The Affordable Care Act defines part-time workers as those working fewer than thirty hours a week. Warning: this definition may change as regulations are issued by the Secretary of Health and Human Services. Section 1513 of the law says the Secretary will issue rules to determine who is full time and who is part time in the cases of employees who are not paid hourly. Stay tuned.

Promotores: Defined by HHS as "trusted local people who serve as community health workers," promotores, the Obama administration recently announced, will be trained by a National Steering Committee to bring benefits to underserved groups.[9]

Public Option: Beginning in 2014, the law requires the federal government to offer two "national plans" available in all fifty state insurance exchanges. One must be not-for-profit. The plans will be designed and managed by the Office of Personnel Management, which administers the civil service, and the plans will have to obey fewer rules than other competing plans. They will have a more flexible loss ratio and looser restrictions on what the plans can cost and how much profit they make.

Rating Bands: Before the Obama health law, insurers in many states gave young people a big price break. The average twenty-five-year-old man uses only about a quarter as much health care as a fifty-five-year-old man. But the Obama health law compels insurers to stay within certain rating bands, which limit the price break that young people can get. The idea is to compel young people to subsidize the cost of care for the middle aged. The two escapes for young adults are to stay on their parent's policy or sign up for a high-deductible plan allowed only for people under thirty.

Reasonable Break Time for Nursing Mothers: Section 4207 of the Obama health law amends Section 7 of the Fair Labor Standards Act to require employers to provide a reasonable break time for an employee to express breast milk for her nursing child for up to one year after the child's birth. The employer must also provide a space, other than a bathroom, that is shielded from view and free from intrusion by co-workers and the public.

Refund Offset: This is the only IRS collection method allowed under the Obama health law. The government may not use liens, issue levies and other penalties, or institute criminal proceedings against those who fail to enroll in a "qualified plan" or pay the penalty. Eventually people will realize that if they don't have a refund coming, the government can't collect the penalties. Thus some people may adjust their tax withholding to avoid a refund.

Secretary of Health and Human Services (HHS): Aside from the President of the United States, this is the person who will be making all the important decisions about your health: what your plan covers, what you have to pay, even what your doctor can do to treat you. In the first six months after the law was passed, 4,105 pages of new regulations were issued,[10] mostly from Health and Human Services and the new commissions, boards, and panels that report to the Secretary of HHS. There are over a thousand places where the law says, "The Secretary shall. . . ."

Self-Employed: If you work for yourself, you will be eligible to buy the mandatory coverage on the exchange in your state.

Small Business Tax Credits: The new law offers tax credits to small businesses to offer health insurance, provided the employer covers at least 50 percent of the premium for the worker (not necessarily for family coverage). To qualify for the full credit (35 percent of the employer's cost), the business must have ten or fewer workers and an average salary not higher than $25,000. The rules change in 2013, and the program ends altogether in 2016. Few businesses have responded. According to a survey by the Small Business and Entrepreneurship Council, reported in *Forbes Magazine*, nearly 90 percent of small businesses surveyed had not applied for the tax credit.[11] The rules are rigid, the credit declines if a business expands beyond ten employees, and employers may worry about how to pay for coverage once the program expires.

Stimulus Legislation: The American Recovery and Reinvestment Act, enacted by the 111th Congress in February 2009, contained several provisions that paved the way for the Obama health law. The most important was a $25.8 billion allocation to provide health information technology for doctors and hospitals.

Subsidies: In 2014, you will be required to enroll in a "qualified" health plan with the benefits the government deems essential. To make this requirement less onerous, the federal government (at taxpayers' expense) will offer subsidies to individuals and households making between 133 and 400 percent of the federal poverty line. Your subsidy will be paid directly to your health plan when you enroll through the exchange in your state.

Tanning Salons: The first of eighteen new taxes or tax hikes under the law is on tanning services. You or the tanning salon owner pays a 10 percent tax on all services sold, as of July 1, 2010.

Temporary High-Risk Pool: Obamacare creates a national temporary high-risk pool to sell insurance to people with pre-existing conditions who have been uninsured for at least six months. Applications were accepted starting in July 1, 2010, with coverage beginning a month later. All U.S. citizens and legal residents are eligible. This is a temporary program, and enrollees are expected to purchase coverage on the state exchanges beginning in 2014. The health law allocates $5 billion to fund the program.

Uninsured: According to the 2010 U.S. Census, 49.9 million people say they are uninsured. But 14 million of them are already eligible for government programs such as Medicaid or CHIP (for children) and haven't signed up. Another 7.6 million have household incomes over $75,000. That leaves about 28.3 million people who probably cannot afford insurance. About 18 million of them are American citizens.

U.S. Preventive Services Task Force (USPSTF): Section 4105(a) of the Obama health law empowers the Secretary of Health and Human Services to "modify or eliminate" certain preventive services for seniors based on the recommendations of the USPSTF. This panel of primary care providers including physicians, nurses, and behavioral health experts was founded in 1984. It has come under criticism in recent years for recommending less use of cancer screening techniques, including mammograms, on healthy and older patients. In 2012, the USPSTF recommended against PSA screening for prostate cancer.

Immediately the prostate cancer experts at the James Buchanan Brady Urological Institute at Johns Hopkins issued a warning that the USPSTF recommendation "sets the clock back to before the 1990s, when 'healthy men' were diagnosed with cancer that was palpable and often, too late for a cure." Early diagnosis, say the Hopkins experts, is "everything." Because of PSA tests, deaths from prostate cancer have plummeted 40 percent since the 1990s, and are now rare. The Hopkins experts pointed out that the USPSTF "had no urologists or other prostate cancer experts. Rather it was composed of individuals with little or no knowledge of the disease. . . ." There is more information on this controversy at the website of the James Buchanan Brady Urological Institute at Johns Hopkins.[12]

W-2: The federal form that employers send you stating your gross pay and deductions. Starting in 2012, box 12 will include the value of your employer-provided health insurance. That will help the IRS verify that you have qualified coverage. The value will not be considered taxable income.

Waivers: These are exemptions from parts of the Obama health law granted at the pleasure of the executive branch. Before 2011, the Obama administration granted 1,472 waivers to certain companies and unions, allowing them not to comply with the new law barring low annual caps and lifetime caps on what insurance companies will pay when an enrollee becomes ill. Recently, the Obama administration considered but denied Catholic institutions such as hospitals and schools an exemption from the employer mandate requirement that all employers, even Catholics, provide coverage for contraception, sterilization, and morning after pills for their workers. Though the law does not empower the executive branch to exempt some people from these aspects of the law, the administration is taking the stand that it has the authority to do so. Critics say the administration's approach turns the rule of law into rule by waivers and favoritism.

AFTERWORD

Replacing the Obama Health Law with Something Better

There is a better way to help the uninsured than Obamacare. Every day, Americans tell me they want a health care bill written in plain English. They want members of Congress to read it before voting on it. And they want a bill that helps make insurance affordable and fair, without the federal government bludgeoning doctors and patients into accepting one-size-fits-all medical care.

What we need is a twenty-page bill in plain English that will reduce premiums, help laid-off Americans afford coverage, and stay out of our private medical affairs. Some states have taken smart approaches to lowering costs and expanding access, including helping people with pre-existing conditions. The twenty-page bill summarized below copies the reforms that have worked in those states.

To read the bill in its entirety, plus cost estimates for its implementation, visit betsymccaughey.com.

This Bill Is Not Dangerous to Your Health—or Your Freedom

(Here's what genuine health reform would look like.)

Title I

Title I liberates consumers to buy policies from insurance brokers in other states and puts consumers on notice that the products they buy outside their own state may have different benefits and consumer protections from those required by their state. This title also imposes federal consumer protections on plans sold interstate, to make sure that consumers who have paid their premiums are protected from recission—that is, from being dropped from the plan when they get sick. These federal protections will also guarantee that adult children could stay on their parent's plan until age twenty-six, for an additional premium.

An HMO plan costs a twenty-five-year-old California male $260 a month, while a New Yorker of the same age has to pay $1,228 for a similar plan.[1] This bill would liberate the young New Yorker to buy a plan wherever he can get the best deal.

Title II

Title II provides federal incentives for states to establish medical courts, ensuring quicker, fairer verdicts in medical liability cases and at the same time preserving every litigant's right to trial by jury. Medical courts will be presided over by judges who know the issues, have experience with medical liability, and can distinguish the honest expert witnesses from the charlatan hired guns. Tort law has always been a matter left to the states. This bill does not mandate that states establish medical courts or attempt to federalize tort law. It does provide block grants to states to impose caps on damages—and more importantly, to establish medical courts. Why only cap unjust damage awards when you can go far toward eliminating them with expert medical malpractice judges?

Title III

Title III provides federal incentives for states to establish or improve subsidized high-risk pools to help consumers with pre-existing conditions.

Title IV

Title IV extends the 65 percent COBRA subsidy (from the Consolidated Omnibus Budget Reconciliation Act of 1985) established by the American Recovery and Reinvestment Act of 2009. Democrats and Republicans can find common ground here. COBRA subsidies are not a permanent entitlement, but rather temporary assistance for those who have been laid off. COBRA premiums, which laid-off workers can pay to maintain their health insurance, are costly just when a family is laid low by unemployment. For more than half the uninsured in the United States, being uninsured is a temporary problem. They find another job and have employment-based insurance again within a year. We need to help them in between jobs.

Now when you're told that Obamacare was passed because "something had to be done," you'll know there's a better way to help the uninsured. In the meantime, I hope you find this guide to the new law helpful.

ACKNOWLEDGMENTS

This book pays tribute to the physicians of the past half century who gave us a golden age of medicine. What a gift! It is enabling us to live longer with better quality of life. A half century ago, 1.7 million Americans died each year from heart disease, many at a young age. Now the death toll is less than a quarter that number. Americans can expect to live seven years longer than they could a half century ago, and to enjoy their later years being active, rather than slowed by damaged hearts and arthritic limbs. We are indebted to the remarkable physician-researchers who transformed the experience of aging. I thank them for their dedication to patients and their relentless pursuit of treatments for heart disease and other age-related ailments.

Dr. Jeffrey Borer epitomizes these achievers. I'd like to thank him for what he has done as a physician and researcher. I'd also like to recognize Dr. Joel Kassimir,

Dr. Francis Perrone, Dr. Samuel Guillory, Dr. Tracy Pfeifer, and Dr. Seymour Cohen for insights contributed to this book and to the national health care debate.

I am indebted to talented editors who made my research on health legislation accessible to the public, especially Robert Pollock and Howard Dickman of the *Wall Street Journal*, Adam Brodsky and Mark Cunningham of the *New York Post*, Wes Mann and Terry Jones of *Investor's Business Daily*, and R. Emmett Tyrell of the *American Spectator*. Also deserving recognition are the radio and television professionals who have informed their audiences about the Obama health law: Neil Cavuto, Larry Kudlow, Andrew Murray, Tom Marr, Lars Larsen, Dennis Miller, William O'Shaughnessy, Frank Marano, Bob Grant, David Asman, and Monica Crowley.

For assistance in getting this book to you—the reader—only two months after the presidential election, I'd like to thank my colleague and friend Amber Christian, my agent Alexander Hoyt, and the editors at Regnery Publishing—Harry Crocker, Elizabeth Kantor, and Maria Ruhl. I am grateful to Donald and Barbara Tober, Ken and Frayda Levy, Mimi Prentice, Randy Kendrick, and others who generously supported my research. Finally, a very personal thanks to Charles H. Brunie, whose character, devotion to liberty, and words of encouragement inspire me day after day.

Betsy McCaughey, Ph.D.
New York, New York 2012

NOTES

Chapter 1

1. Sandy Kleffman, "Nurses Walk Off the Job Thursday at Seven East Bay Hospitals Affiliated with Sutter Health," *San Jose Mercury News*, November 1, 2012.
2. James Sherk, "Obamacare Will Price Skilled Workers Out of Full-Time Jobs," WebMemo on Healthcare, Heritage Foundation, October 11, 2011, www.heritage.org.
3. Shobban Singhal, et al., "How U.S. Health Care Reform Will Affect Employee Benefits," *McKinsey Quarterly*, June 2, 2011.
4. Vivian Y. Wu and Yu-Chu Chen, "The Long Term Impact of Medicare Payment Reductions on Patient Outcomes," National Bureau of Economic Research Working Paper 16859, March 2011.

Chapter 4

1. Fred Lucas, "Obama Cabinet Secretary: 'The Private Market Is in a Death Spiral,'" CNSNews.com, February 29, 2012.
2. Goldwater Institute lawsuit challenging the Patient Protection and Affordable Care Act.

Chapter 5

1. Betsy McCaughey, "How ObamaCare Destroys Your Privacy," *New York Post*, June 15, 2011.

Chapter 6

1. Singhal, "How U.S. Health Care Reform Will Affect Employee Benefits."
2. James Sherk, WebMemo on Healthcare.
3. Ibid.
4. Dan Danner, president and CEO of the National Federation of Independent Businesses, "NFIB: Mandate Ends Vital Freedoms," *USA Today*, June 28, 2012.
5. Elise Viebeck, "HealthWatch," *The Hill*, July 24, 2012.
6. Singhal, "How U.S. Health Care Reform Will Affect Employer Benefits"
7. Linda J. Blumberg, Matthew Buettgens, Judy Feder, and John Holahan, "Why Employers Will Continue to Provide Health Insurance: The Impact of the Affordable Care Act," Urban Institute, October 26, 2011; Lisa Dubay, John Holahan, Sharon K. Long, and Emily Lawton, "Will the Affordable Care Act Be a Job Killer?" Urban Institute, October 22, 2012.
8. Julie Jargon, "Chili's Feels Heat to Pare Costs," *Wall Street Journal*, January 28, 2011.
9. Congressional Budget Office, "The Budget and Economic Outlook: An Update," August 18, 2010, Testimony of CBO Director Douglas Elmendorf before the House Budget Committee, U.S. House of Representatives, February 10, 2011.
10. Grady Payne, testimony before the Subcommittee on Healthcare, Committee on Oversight and Reform, U.S. House of Representatives, July 28, 2011.
11. James Sherk, WebMemo on Healthcare.

Chapter 7

1. Jackie Farwell, "LePage Won't 'Lift a Finger' to Set Up Maine's Health Insurance Exchange," *Bangor Daily News*, November 15, 2012.
2. Howard K. Koh, Garth Graham, and Sherry A. Glied, "Reducing Racial and Ethnic Disparities: The Action Plan from the Depart-

ment of Health and Human Services," *Health Affairs* 30, no. 1, (October 2011).

Chapter 8

1. Edmund F. Haislmaier and Brian Blase, "Obamacare: Impact on States," Heritage Foundation, July 1, 2010.
2. Ibid.
3. Edward Miller, "Health Reform Could Harm Medicaid Patients," *Wall Street Journal*, December 4, 2009.
4. D. J. LaPar, et al., "Primary Payer Status Affects Mortality," *Annals of Internal Medicine* 252 (2010): 3; Avik Roy, "The Urgency of Medicaid Reform," thehealthcareblog.com, March 9, 2011.
5. Michael A. Gaglia Jr., et al., "Effect of Insurance Type on Adverse Cardiac Events after Percutaneou Coronary Intervention," *Journal of the American College of Cardiology* 107:5, 675–80. For an excellent review of studies on Medicaid outcomes, see Scott Gottlieb, "Medicaid Is Worse than No Coverage at All," *Wall Street Journal*, March 10, 2011.
6. The best review of these studies is Brian Blase, "Medicaid Provides Poor Quality Care: What the Research Shows," Heritage Foundation, May 5, 2011.
7. Paul R. Houchens, "ACA Impact on Premium Rates in the Individual and Small Group Markets," Milliman Health Care Exchange Issue Brief: Indiana Exchange Policy Committee, June 2011.

Chapter 10

1. Karen M. Beauregard, "Persons Denied Private Health Coverage Due to Poor Health," Agency for Health Care Policy & Research, Report No. 92-0016, December 1991. Only adults purchasing health coverage in the individual market can be denied coverage, and that is a tiny fraction of all those covered.

2. "Coverage of Uninsurable Pre-Existing Conditions: State and Federal High Risk Pools," National Conference of State Legislatures, updated October 2012.
3. Sean P. Keehan, et al., "National Health Expenditure Projections," *Health Affairs*, 31:7 (July 2012), pp. 1600–1610.

Chapter 11

1. Andrea M. Sisko, et al., "National Health Expenditure Projections," *Health Affairs*, October 2010, 1933–41.
2. Richard S. Foster, "The Financial Outlook for Medicare," Testimony before the House Committee on the Budget," July 13, 2011; Kaiser Health News, July 14, 2011.
3. Vivan Wu and Yu-Chu Shen, "The Long Term Impact of Medicare Payment Reductions on Patient Outcomes," National Bureau of Economic Research, working paper no. 16859, March 2011.
4. Peter Orszag, "Health Costs Are the Real Deficit Threat: That's Why President Obama Is Making Health-Care Reform a Priority," *Wall Street Journal*, May 15, 2009. Dartmouth Atlas White Paper, December, 2008.
5. John E. Wennberg, et al., "Improving Quality and Curbing Health Care Spending," *Dartmouth Atlas of Health Care 2008*.
6. John A. Romley, et al., "Hospital Spending and Inpatient Mortality," *Archives of Internal Medicine* 154:3 (February 1, 2011).
7. President Barack Obama, "Remarks by the President in ABC 'Prescription for America' Town Hall on Health Care," White House Office of the Press Secretary, June 25, 2009.
8. Peter Cram, et al., "Total Knee Arthroplasty Volume, Utilization, and Outcomes among Medicare Beneficiaries, 1991–2012," *Journal of the American Medical Association* 308:12 (September 26, 2012).
9. Dr. Seymour Cohen, statement at the October 19, 2009 forum at the Grand Hyatt Hotel, New York City.

10. "Comparison of Projected Enrollment in Medicare Advantage Plans and Subsidies for Extra Benefits Not Covered by Medicare Under Current Law and Under Reconciliation Legislation Combined with H.R. 3590 as Passed by the Senate," the Congressional Budget Office, March 19, 2010. See also Foster, "Estimated Financial Effects."
11. "Text: Obama's AMA Speech on Health Care," CBSNews.com, June 15, 2009.
12. Foster, "Estimated Financial Effects"; Douglas Elmendorf, letter to Jeff Sessions, United States Senate, January 22, 2010.
13. Ibid. Closing the donut hole will cost $12 billion from 2010 through 2019.

Chapter 12

1. Treasury Inspector General for Administration J. Russell George, press release, "The IRS Has Made Significant Progress in Planning for the Implementation of the Affordable Care Act," October 24, 2011.
2. J. Russell George, Inspector General, Memorandum for Secretary Geithner, "Management and Performance Challenges Facing the Internal Revenue Service for Fiscal Year 2012," p. 12.
3. Joint Committee on Taxation, estimate updated as of July 2012, reported by William McBride, "Obamacare Taxes Now Estimated to Cost $1 Trillion over 10 Years," Tax Foundation, July 25, 2012.
4. Congressional Budget Office, letter to the Honorable Evan Bayh, November 30, 2009; Joint Committee on Taxation, letter to the Honorable Jon Kyl, May 12, 2011.
5. Congressional Budget Office, "Estimates for the Insurance Coverage Provisions of the Affordable Care Act Updated for the Recent Supreme Court Decision," July 23 2012, Table 4. (The employer mandate was projected to yield $117 billion and the individual mandate penalty to yield $55 billion.)

6. Congressional Budget Office, Letter to the Honorable John Boehner, July 23, 2012.
7. Ricardo Alonso-Zaldivar and Andrew Taylor, "Budget Office: Obama's Health Law Reduces Deficit," StarTribune.com, July 24, 2012.
8. Keehan, "National Health Expenditure Projections."
9. "Hoyer: New CBO Report Confirms Health Care Law Controls Costs, Reduces Deficit," press release, http://www.democraticwhip.gov/content/hoyer-new-cbo-report-confirms-health-care-law-controls-costs-reduces-deficit.

Chapter 13

1. Emily P. Walker, "AMA Makes Small Gain in Membership," *MedPage Today*, June 17, 2012.
2. Parija Kavilanz, "Doctors Going Broke," CNN.com, January 5, 2012.
3. Marc Siegel, "Will Your Doctor Quit? ObamaCare Foretells Mass Exodus from Patient Care," *Forbes*, August 12, 2012.
4. Hal Scherz, "Doctors Drowning in Alphabet Soup," Townhall.com, March 8, 2011.
5. David Blumenthal, "Stimulating the Adoption of Health Information Technology," *New England Journal of Medicine*, April 9, 2009.

Chapter 14

1. Statement by Gloria Feldt, president of Planned Parenthood Federation of America, June 5, 2003.
2. *Coons v. Geithner*, No. 2-10-cv-01714-ECV, complaint filed in the District Court of Arizona on August 12, 2010.
3. Adam Liptak, "Religious Groups Given 'Exception' to Work Bias Law," *New York Times*, January 11, 2012; David Skeel, "On Religious Freedom, Years of Battle Ahead," *Wall Street Journal*, January 27, 2012.

4. Testimony before the House Energy and Commerce Subcommittee on Health, July 13, 2011.

Chapter 15

1. Sean P. Keehan, et al., "National Expenditure Projections," *Health Affairs*, June 11, 2012.
2. Tarren Bragdon, "Rx NY: A Prescription for More Accessible Health Care in NY," Empire Center for New York State Policy, December 11, 2007.
3. Nancy-Ann DeParle, "One Year of the Affordable Care Act," White House Blog, March 23, 2009.
4. Robert Steinbrook, "Saying No Isn't NICE: The Travails of Britain's National Institute for Health and Clinical Excellence," *New England Journal of Medicine*, 359 (November 6, 2008), 1977–1981.
5. Mark W. Stanton, "The High Concentration of U.S. Health Care Expenditures," Agency for Healthcare Research and Quality, Research in Action, issue 19, June 2006.
6. Ezekiel Emanuel and Victor Fuchs, "The Perfect Storm of Overutilization," *Journal of the American Medical Association* 299: 23 (June 18, 2008), 2789–2791.
7. Congressional Budget Office, "Key Issues in Analyzing Major Health Insurance Proposals," December 18, 2008, publication 41746; Congressional Budget Office, "Technological Change and the Growth of Health Care Spending, January 31, 2008.
8. David Cutler and Mark McClellan, "Is Technological Change in Medicine Worth It?" *Health Affairs* 20: 5 (September 2001) 11–29.
9. Kathleen Sebelius, "Sebelius Statement on New Medicare Trustees Report," press release, U.S. Department of Health and Human Services, May 12, 2009.
10. Council of Economic Advisors, "The Economic Case for Health Care Reform," released June 2, 2009, published by the White House.

11. U. W. Reinhart, et al., “US Health in an International Context,” *Health Affairs*, 23:3 (March 2004), 10–25.
12. David Blumenthal, “Controlling Health Care Expenditures,” *New England Journal of Medicine*, 344 (March 8, 2001), 766–69.
13. Transcript of Meet the Press, Tom Daschle guest, August 16, 2009, available at www.msnbc.msn.com.
14. Transcript of *Larry King Live*, CNN, August 12, 2009.
15. The *Tampa Bay Times* operates a website called PolitiFact. Even now it repeats the WHO 37th-place ranking and uses it to rebut the claims that the U.S. has superior health care. For example, it cited the now twelve-year-old WHO report on July 9, 2012, to rebut Speaker of the House John Boehner and again on August 30, 2012, to refute New Jersey Governor Chris Christie’s statement that health care is best in the U.S.
16. World Health Organization, “The World Health Report 2000.”
17. Letter of Philip Musgrove to the *New England Journal of Medicine* 362 (April 22, 2010), 1546–47.
18. Francis Berrno, et al., “Survival for Eight Major Cancers and All Cancers Combined for European Adults Diagnosed in 1995–99: Results of the EUROCARE-4 Study,” *Lancet Oncology* 8: 9 (September 2007) 773–83.

Conclusion

1. National Institutes of health fact sheets on heart disease available on the NIH website, http://health.nih.gov/see_all_topics.aspx.
2. Barack Obama, “News Conference by the President,” White House Office of the Press Secretary, July 23, 2009. See the transcript of the press conference at http://www.whitehouse.gov/the-press-office/news-conference-president-july-22-2009.
3. “Text: Obama’s Health Care Town Hall in Portsmouth,” *New York Times*, August 11, 2009.
4. Statement of the American College of Surgeons, August 12, 2009.

Glossary

1. Howard K. Koh, Garth Graham, and Sherry A. Glied, "Reducing Racial and Ethnic Disparities: The Action Plan from the Department of Health and Human Services." *Health Affairs* 30: 10 (October 2011). The authors call for increased taxpayer funding to meet the needs of undocumented immigrants at the community health centers.
2. Douglas W. Elmendorf, Congressional Budget Office, letter to Senator Harry Reid, November 18, 2009.
3. Community Transformation Grant (CTG) Program Fact Sheet, Centers for Disease Control and Prevention, http://www.cdc.gov/communitytransformation/funds/index.htm. All other information about Community Health Councils was found on the organization's website at www.chc-inc.org.
4. For the administration's statements that the loans will not be repaid, see "HealthWatch," *The Hill*, July 18, 2011. For an updated list of recipients, see the HHS website. For a sample of press coverage on the loans, see Andrea K. Walker, "U.S. Loan to Kick-Start Md. Insurance Co-op," *Baltimore Sun*, September 29, 2012; "CMS Awards Two Co-op Loans," American Hospital Association press release, September 4, 2012; "Western States Lead the Way on Healthcare COOP Development," *Business Wire*, August 8, 2012; Senator Michael F. Bennet (Democrat, Colorado) press release, "Bennet Applauds Announcement of $69 Million Loan for Colorado Health Insurance Cooperative," July 27, 2012.
5. Jordan Fabian, "Obama Healthcare Plan Nixes Ben Nelson's Cornhusker Kickback Deal," *The Hill*, February 22, 2010; Reuters, "Obama Plan Kills Cornhusker Kickback, Boosts Medicaid," February 22, 2010.
6. Koh, "Reducing Racial and Ethnic Disparities."
7. Peter Suderman, "ObamaCare's Early Retiree Benefits Program," Reason.com, April 1, 2011.

8. Philip Klein, "New Menu Regulations Eat into Profits for Small Businesses," *Washington Examiner*, August 9, 2011.
9. Koh, Graham, and Glied, "Reducing Racial and Ethnic Disparities."
10. Congressional Research Service, December 10, 2010.
11. Sally Pipes, "Small-Business Health Care Tax Credits Are Having a Minuscule Impact," *Forbes*, July 4, 2011.
12. Patrick C. Walsh, "Response to the United States Preventive Services Task Force (USPSTF) Recommendation against PSA Testing for the Early Diagnosis of Prostate Cancer in Healthy Men," James Buchanan Brady Urological Institute, Johns Hopkins Medicine, no date, http://www.urology.jhu.edu/PSA_controversy.php.

Afterword

1. See ehealthinsurance.com.

INDEX